SHOE DOG

SHOE DOG

A MEMOIR BY THE CREATOR OF *NIKE*

YOUNG READERS EDITION

PHIL KNIGHT

Simon & Schuster Books for Young Readers

NEW YORK   LONDON   TORONTO   SYDNEY   NEW DELHI

SIMON & SCHUSTER BOOKS FOR YOUNG READERS
An imprint of Simon & Schuster Children's Publishing Division
1230 Avenue of the Americas, New York, New York 10020

SIMON & SCHUSTER BOOKS FOR YOUNG READERS
is a trademark of Simon & Schuster, Inc.
For information about special discounts for bulk purchases, please contact
Simon & Schuster Special Sales at 1-866-506-1949 or business@simonandschuster.com.
The Simon & Schuster Speakers Bureau can bring authors to your live event.
For more information or to book an event, contact the Simon & Schuster Speakers Bureau
at 1-866-248-3049 or visit our website at www.simonspeakers.com.
Also available in a Simon & Schuster Books for Young Readers hardcover edition
Interior design by Hilary Zarycky
Cover design by Krista Vossen
The text for this book was set in Adobe Jenson Pro.
Manufactured in the United States of America
1124 MTN
This Simon & Schuster Books for Young Readers paperback edition August 2019
12 14 16 18 20 19 17 15 13 11
The Library of Congress has cataloged the hardcover edition as follows:
Names: Knight, Philip H., 1938– author.
Title: Shoe dog : young readers edition / Phil Knight.
Description: New York : Simon & Schuster/Paula Wiseman Books, 2017. |
Audience: Grade 4 to 6.
Identifiers: LCCN 2017007594| ISBN 9781534401181 (hardback) |
ISBN 9781534401198 (paperback) | ISBN 9781534401204 (eBook)
Subjects: LCSH: Knight, Philip H., 1938– | Nike (Firm) | Businesspeople—United
States—Biography—Juvenile literature. | Sporting goods industry—United States—
History—Juvenile literature. | BISAC:
JUVENILE NONFICTION / Biography & Autobiography / General. | JUVENILE
NONFICTION / Business & Economics. | JUVENILE NONFICTION / Sports &
Recreation / General.
Classification: LCC HD9992.U52 K555 2017 | DDC 338.7/68536 [B]—dc23
LC record available at https://lccn.loc.gov/2017007594

For my grandchildren, so they will know

In the beginner's mind there are many possibilities,
but in the expert's mind there are few.
—SHUNRYU SUZUKI, *Zen Mind, Beginner's Mind*

INTRODUCTION

Letter to My Grandchildren

Dear Jordan, Logan, Ridley, Willow, Anthony, Dylan, Nicholas, Reade, Henry, Riley, and Merrick,

When I was in high school, I had no idea what I wanted to do with my life. Or, more precisely, I wanted to do something different every week—journalist, businessman, lawyer, sports announcer, teacher . . .

And it didn't get a lot better through college and graduate school. I tried to get a good education—I knew that would be a help—but it worried me to have to make real life choices.

I now realize I was lucky. The decision-making process is an enjoyable part of the journey. There was, for me, not a clear path, but one that worked out pretty well, and it has occurred to me that sharing this journey with you might be helpful.

I can remember, for the most of you, the moment of your birth—when all the world lay before you. And with that a challenge for all your older relatives: how to prepare you, how to educate you, how to discipline you, how to smile with you.

But in the normal course, and all too soon, there comes

a day when we will go into your room, now turned cold, and there is only an empty bed with no impression from a human body. Our work done, you will have gone to a grown-up world of college or work or life with someone else.

If any of the experiences or lessons learned on your grandfather's journey are helpful . . . well, then it will have all been worthwhile.

My own house was somewhat different than the one in which you grew up. In my house my sons Matt and Travis, the fathers of six of you, grew up with a third brother— one they could not see or touch but whose presence was constant.

And they always knew that other brother was there.

It became important to me that you know that member of the family. Oh, there has been plenty written about him, but I wanted you to see him through my eyes—his birth, his teenage struggles, his growth into that time when he, too, could leave home.

I have shown him here with all his youthful imperfections, but through it all I hope you accept him as a member of the family.

With lots of love,

Papa

SHOE DOG

Dawn

I was up before the others, before the birds, before the sun. I wolfed down a piece of toast, put on my shorts and sweatshirt, and laced up my green running shoes. Then slipped quietly out the back door.

I stretched my legs, my hamstrings, my lower back, and groaned as I took the first few balky steps down the cool road, into the fog. Why is it always so hard to get started?

There were no cars, no people, no signs of life. I was all alone, the world to myself—though the trees seemed oddly aware of me. Then again, this was Oregon. The trees always seemed to know. The trees always had your back.

What a beautiful place to be from, I thought, gazing around. Calm, green, tranquil—I was proud to call Oregon my home, proud to call little Portland my place of birth. But I felt a stab of regret, too. Though beautiful, Oregon struck some people as the kind of place where nothing big had ever happened, or was ever likely to. If we Oregonians were famous for anything, it was an old, old trail we'd had to blaze to get here. Since then, things had been pretty tame.

The best teacher I ever had, one of the finest men I ever knew, spoke of that trail often. It's our birthright, he'd growl. Our character, our fate—our DNA. "The cowards never started," he'd tell me, "and the weak died along the way—that leaves us."

Us. Some rare strain of pioneer spirit was discovered along that trail, my teacher believed, some outsize sense of possibility mixed with a diminished capacity for pessimism—and it was our job as Oregonians to keep that strain alive.

I'd nod, showing him all due respect. I loved the guy. But walking away I'd sometimes think: Jeez, it's just a dirt road.

That foggy morning I'd recently blazed my own trail—back home, after seven long years away. It was strange being home again. Stranger still was living again with my parents and twin sisters, sleeping in my childhood bed. Late at night I'd lie on my back, staring at my college textbooks, my high school trophies and blue ribbons, thinking: This is me? *Still?*

I moved quicker down the road. My breath formed rounded, frosty puffs, swirling into the fog. I savored that first physical awakening, that brilliant moment before the mind is fully clear, when the limbs and joints first begin to loosen and the material body starts to melt away. Solid to liquid.

Faster, I told myself. Faster.

On paper, I thought, I'm an adult. Graduated from a good college—University of Oregon. Earned a master's from a top business school—Stanford. Survived a yearlong hitch in the U.S. Army—Fort Lewis and Fort Eustis. My résumé said I was a learned, accomplished soldier, a twenty-four-year-old man in full. . . . So why, I wondered, why do I still feel like a kid?

Like the same shy, pale, rail-thin kid I'd always been.

Maybe because I still hadn't experienced anything of life. Least of all its many temptations and excitements. I hadn't broken a rule. The 1960s were just under way, the age of rebellion, and I was the only person in America who hadn't yet rebelled. I couldn't think of one time I'd done the unexpected.

If I tended to dwell on all the things I wasn't, the reason was simple. Those were the things I knew best. I'd have found it difficult to say what or who exactly I was, or might become. Like all my friends, I wanted to be successful. Unlike my friends I didn't know what that meant. Money? Maybe. Family? House? Sure, if I was lucky. These were the goals I was taught to aspire to, and part of me did aspire to them, instinctively. But deep down I was searching for something else, something more. I had an aching sense that our time is short, shorter than we ever know, short as a morning run, and I wanted mine to be meaningful. And purposeful. And creative. And important. Above all . . . different.

I wanted to leave a mark on the world.

I wanted to win.

No, that's not right. I simply didn't want to lose.

And then it happened. As my young heart began to thump, as my pink lungs expanded like the wings of a bird, as the trees turned to greenish blurs, I saw it all before me, exactly what I wanted my life to be. Play.

Yes, I thought, that's it. That's the word. The secret of happiness, I'd always suspected, lay somewhere in that moment when the ball is in midair, when both boxers sense the approach of the bell, when the runners near the finish line and the crowd rises as one. There's a kind of exuberant clarity in that pulsing half second before winning and losing are decided. I wanted that, whatever that was, to be my life, my daily life.

At different times I'd fantasized about becoming a great novelist, a great journalist, a great statesman. But the ultimate dream was always to be a great athlete. Sadly, fate had made me good, not great. At twenty-four I was finally resigned to that fact. I'd run track at Oregon, and I'd distinguished myself, lettering three of four years. But that was that, the end. Now, as I began to clip off one brisk six-minute mile after another, as the rising sun set fire to the lowest needles of the pines, I asked myself: What if there were a way, without being an athlete, to feel what athletes feel? To play all the time, instead of working? Or else to enjoy work so much that it becomes essentially the same thing?

The world was so overrun, the daily grind was so exhausting and often unjust—maybe the only answer, I thought, was to find some prodigious, improbable dream that seemed worthy, that seemed fun, that seemed a good fit, and chase it with an athlete's single-minded dedication and purpose. Like it or not, life is a game. Whoever denies that truth, whoever simply refuses to play, gets left on the sidelines, and I didn't want that. More than anything, that was the thing I did not want.

Which led, as always, to my Crazy Idea. Maybe, I thought, just maybe, I need to take one more look at my Crazy Idea. Maybe my Crazy Idea just might . . . work?

Maybe.

No, no, I thought, running faster, faster, running as if I were chasing someone *and* being chased all at the same time. It *will* work. By God, I'll *make* it work. No maybes about it.

I was suddenly smiling. Almost laughing. Drenched in sweat, moving as gracefully and effortlessly as I ever had, I saw my Crazy Idea shining up ahead, and it didn't look all that crazy. It didn't even look like an idea. It looked like a place. It looked like a person, or some life force that existed long before I did, separate from me, but also part of me. Waiting for me, but also hiding from me. That might sound a little high-flown, a little *crazy*. But that's how I felt back then.

Or maybe I didn't. Maybe my memory is enlarging this eureka moment, or condensing many eureka moments into one. Or maybe, if there was such a moment, it was nothing more than runner's high. I don't know. I can't say. So much about those days, and the months and years into which they slowly sorted themselves, has vanished, like those rounded, frosty puffs of breath.

What remains, however, is this one comforting certainty, this one anchoring truth that will never go away. At twenty-four I *did* have a Crazy Idea, and somehow, despite being dizzy with existential angst, and fears about the future, and doubts about myself, as all young men and women in their midtwenties are, I *did* decide that the world is made up of crazy ideas. History is one long processional of crazy ideas. The things I loved most—books, sports, democracy, free enterprise—started as crazy ideas.

For that matter, few ideas are as crazy as my favorite thing, running. It's hard. It's painful. It's risky. The rewards are few and far from guaranteed. When you run around an oval track, or down an empty road, you have no real destination. At least, none that can fully justify the effort. The act itself becomes the destination. It's not just that there's no finish line; it's that you define the finish line. Whatever pleasures or gains you derive from the act of running, you must find them within. It's all in how you frame it, how you sell it to yourself. Every runner knows this. You run and run, mile after mile, and you never quite know why. You tell yourself that you're running toward some goal, chasing some rush, but really you run because the alternative, stopping, scares you to death.

So that morning in 1962 I told myself: Let everyone else call your idea crazy . . . just keep going. Don't stop. Don't even think about stopping until you get there, and don't give much thought to where "there" is. Whatever comes, just don't stop.

That's the precocious, prescient, urgent advice I managed to give myself, out of the blue, and somehow managed to take. Half a century later, I believe it's the best advice—maybe the only advice—any of us should ever give.

Part One

Now, *here*, you see, it takes all the running *you* can do, to keep in the same place. If you want to get somewhere else, you must run at least twice as fast as that.

—LEWIS CARROLL, *Through the Looking-Glass*

1962

When I broached the subject with my father, when I worked up the nerve to speak to him about my Crazy Idea, I made sure it was in the early evening. That was always the best time with Dad. He was relaxed then, well fed, stretched out in his vinyl recliner in the TV nook. I can still tilt back my head and close my eyes and hear the sound of the audience laughing, the tinny theme songs of his favorite shows, *Wagon Train* and *Rawhide*.

His all-time favorite was *The Red Buttons Show* from the 1950s. Every episode began with Red singing: *Ho ho, hee hee . . . strange things are happening.*

I set a straight-backed chair beside him and gave a wan smile and waited for the next commercial. I'd rehearsed my spiel, in my head, over and over, especially the opening. *Sooo, Dad, you remember that Crazy Idea I had at Stanford . . . ?*

It was one of my final classes, a seminar on entrepreneurship. I'd written a research paper about shoes, and the paper had evolved from a run-of-the-mill assignment to an all-out obsession. Being a runner, I knew something about running shoes. Being a business buff, I knew that Japanese cameras had made deep cuts into the camera market, which had once been dominated by Germans. Thus, I argued in my paper that Japanese running shoes might do the same thing. The idea interested me, then inspired me, then captivated me. It seemed so obvious, so simple, so potentially huge.

I'd spent weeks and weeks on that paper. I'd moved into the library, devoured everything I could find about importing and exporting, about starting a company. Finally, as required, I'd given a formal presentation of the paper to my classmates, who reacted with formal boredom. Not one asked a single question. They greeted my passion and intensity with labored sighs and vacant stares.

The professor thought my Crazy Idea had merit: He gave me an A. But that was that. At least, that was supposed to be that. I'd never really stopped thinking about that paper. Through the rest of my time at Stanford, through every morning run and right up to that moment in the TV nook, I'd pondered going to Japan, finding a shoe company, pitching *them* my Crazy Idea, in the hopes that they'd have a more enthusiastic reaction than my classmates, that they'd want to partner with a shy, pale, rail-thin kid from sleepy Oregon.

I'd also toyed with the notion of making an exotic detour

on my way to and from Japan. How can I leave my mark on the world, I thought, unless I get out there first and *see* it? Before running a big race, you always want to walk the track. A back-packing trip around the globe might be just the thing. I wanted to visit the planet's most beautiful and wondrous places.

And its most sacred. Of course I wanted to taste other foods, hear other languages, dive into other cultures, but what I really craved was "connection" with a capital "C." I wanted to experience what the Chinese call Tao, the Greeks call Logos, the Hindus call Jñāna, the Buddhists call Dharma. What the Christians call Spirit. Before setting out on my own personal life voyage, I thought, let me first understand the greater voyage of humankind. Let me explore the grandest temples and churches and shrines, the holiest rivers and mountaintops. Let me feel the presence of . . . God?

Yes, I told myself, yes. For want of a better word, God.

But first, I'd need my father's approval. More, I'd need his cash.

I'd already mentioned making a big trip, the previous year, and my father seemed open to it. But surely he'd forgotten. And surely I was pushing it, adding to the original proposal this Crazy Idea, this outrageous side trip—to Japan? To launch a company? Talk about boondoggles.

Surely he'd see this as a bridge too far.

And a bridge too darned expensive. I had some savings

from the Army and from various part-time jobs over the last several summers. On top of which, I planned to sell my car, a cherry-black 1960 MG with racing tires and a twin cam. All of which amounted to fifteen hundred dollars, leaving me a grand short, I now told my father. He nodded, uh-huh, mmhmm, and flicked his eyes from the TV to me and back again, while I laid it all out.

Remember how we talked, Dad? How I said I want to see the world?

The Himalayas? The Pyramids?

The Dead Sea, Dad? The Dead *Sea*?

Well, ha-ha, I'm also thinking of stopping off in Japan, Dad. Remember my Crazy Idea? Japanese running shoes? Right? It could be huge, Dad. Huge.

I was laying it on thick, putting on the hard sell, extra hard, because I always hated selling and because this particular sell had zero chance. My father had just forked out hundreds of dollars to the University of Oregon, thousands more to Stanford. He was the publisher of the *Oregon Journal*, a solid job that paid for all the basic comforts, including our spacious white house on Claybourne Street, in Portland's quietest suburb, Eastmoreland. But the man wasn't made of money.

Also, this was 1962. The earth was bigger then. Though humans were beginning to orbit the planet in capsules, 90 percent of Americans still had never been on an airplane. The average man or woman had never ventured farther than one hundred miles from his or her own front door, so the mere mention of global travel by airplane would unnerve any father, and especially mine, whose predecessor at the paper had died in an air crash.

Setting aside money, setting aside safety concerns, the whole thing was just so impractical. I was aware that twenty-six of twenty-seven new companies failed, and my father was aware, too, and the idea of taking on such a colossal risk went against everything he stood for. In many ways my father was a conventional Episcopalian, a believer in Jesus Christ. But he also worshipped another secret deity—respectability. He liked being admired. He liked doing a vigorous backstroke each day in the mainstream. Going around the world on a lark, therefore, would simply make no sense to him. It wasn't done. Certainly not by the respectable sons of respectable men. It was something other people's kids did.

For these and a dozen other reasons I expected my father to greet my pitch in the TV nook with a furrowed brow and a quick put-down. *Ha-ha, Crazy Idea. Fat chance, Buck.* (My given name was Philip, but my father always called me Buck. In fact, he'd been calling me Buck since before I was born. My mother told me he'd been in the habit of patting her stomach and asking, "How's little Buck today?") As I stopped talking, however, as I stopped pitching, my father rocked forward in his vinyl recliner and shot me a funny look. He said that he always regretted not traveling more when he was young. He said a trip might be just the finishing touch to my education. He said a lot of things, all of them focused more on the trip than the Crazy Idea, but I wasn't about to correct him. I wasn't about to complain, because in sum he was giving his blessing. And his cash.

"Okay," he said. "Okay, Buck. Okay."

I thanked my father and fled the nook before he had a chance to change his mind. Only later did I realize with a spasm of guilt that my father's lack of travel was an ulterior reason, perhaps the main reason, that I wanted to go. This trip, this Crazy Idea, would be one sure way of becoming someone other than him. Someone less respectable.

Or maybe not less respectable. Maybe just less obsessed with respectability.

The rest of the family wasn't quite so supportive. When my grandmother got wind of my itinerary, one item in particular appalled her. "Japan!" she cried. "Why, Buck, what about Pearl Harbor!"

I loved my mother's mother, whom we all called Mom Hatfield. And I understood her fear. Japan was about as far as you could get from Roseburg, Oregon, the farm town where she was born and where she'd lived all her life. I'd spent many summers down there with her and Pop Hatfield. Almost every night we'd sit out on the porch, listening to the croaking bullfrogs compete with the console radio.

My twin sisters, Jeanne and Joanne, four years younger than me, didn't seem to care one way or another where I went or what I did.

And my mother, as I recall, said nothing. She rarely did. But there was something different about her silence this time. It equaled consent. Even pride.

I spent weeks reading, planning, preparing for my trip. I went for long runs, musing on every detail while racing the wild geese as they flew overhead. Their tight V formations—I'd read somewhere that the geese in the rear of the formation, cruising in the backdraft, only have to work 80 percent as hard as the leaders. Every runner understands this. Front-runners always work the hardest, and risk the most.

Long before approaching my father, I'd decided it would be good to have a companion on my trip, and that companion should be my Stanford classmate Carter. Though he'd been a hoops star at William Jewell College, Carter wasn't your typical jock. He wore thick glasses and read books. Good books. He was easy to talk to, and easy not to talk to—equally important qualities in a friend. Essential in a travel companion.

But Carter laughed in my face. When I laid out the list of places I wanted to see—Hawaii, Tokyo, Hong Kong, Rangoon, Calcutta, Bombay, Saigon, Kathmandu, Cairo, Istanbul,

Athens, Jordan, Jerusalem, Nairobi, Rome, Paris, Vienna, West Berlin, East Berlin, Munich, London—he rocked back on his heels and guffawed. Mortified, I looked down and began to make apologies. Then Carter, still laughing, said: "What a swell idea, Buck!"

I looked up. He wasn't laughing at me. He was laughing with joy, with glee. He was impressed. It took nerve to put together an itinerary like that, he said. Courage. He wanted in.

Days later he got the okay from his parents, plus a loan from his father. Carter never did mess around. See an open shot, take it—that was Carter. I told myself there was much I could learn from a guy like that as we circled the earth.

We each packed one suitcase and one backpack. Only the bare necessities, we promised each other. A few pairs of jeans, a few T-shirts. Running shoes, desert boots, sunglasses, plus one pair of "suntans"—the 1960s word for khakis.

I also packed one good suit. A green Brooks Brothers two-button.

Just in case my Crazy Idea came to fruition.

September 7, 1962. Carter and I piled into his battered old Chevy and drove at warp speed down I-5, through the Willamette Valley, out the wooded bottom of Oregon, which felt like plunging through the roots of a tree. We sped into the piney tip of California, up and over tall green mountain passes, then down, down, until long after midnight we swept into fog-cloaked San Francisco. For several days we stayed with some friends, sleeping on their floor, and then we swung by Stanford and fetched a few of Carter's things out of storage. Finally we bought two discounted tickets on Standard Airlines to Honolulu. One-way, eighty bucks.

It felt like only minutes later that Carter and I were stepping onto the sandy tarmac of Oahu's airport. We wheeled and looked at the sky and thought: That is not the sky back home.

We took a cab to Waikiki Beach and checked into a motel directly across the street from the sea. In one motion we dropped our bags and pulled on our swim trunks. Race you to the water!

As my feet hit the sand I whooped and laughed and kicked off my sneakers, then sprinted directly into the waves. I didn't stop until I was up to my neck in the foam. I dove to the bottom, all the way to the bottom, and then came up gasping, laughing, and rolled onto my back. At last I stumbled onto the shore and plopped onto the sand, smiling at the birds and the clouds. I must have looked like an escaped mental patient. Carter, sitting beside me now, wore the same daffy expression.

"We should stay here," I said. "Why be in a hurry to leave?"

"What about The Plan?" Carter said. "Going around the world?"

"Plans change."

Carter grinned. "Swell idea, Buck."

So we got jobs. Selling encyclopedias door-to-door. Not glamorous, to be sure, but heck. We didn't start work until 7:00 p.m., which gave us plenty of time for surfing. Suddenly nothing was more important than learning to surf. After only a few tries I was able to stay upright on a board, and after a few weeks I was good. Really good.

Gainfully employed, we ditched our motel room and signed a lease on an apartment, a furnished studio with two beds, one real, one fake—a sort of ironing board that folded out from the wall. Carter, being longer and heavier, got the real bed, and I got the ironing board. I didn't care. After a day of surfing and selling encyclopedias, I could have slept in a luau fire pit. The rent was one hundred bucks a month, which we split down the middle.

Life was sweet. Life was heaven. Except for one small thing. I couldn't sell encyclopedias.

I couldn't sell encyclopedias to save my life. The older I got, it seemed, the shier I got, and the sight of my extreme discomfort often made strangers uncomfortable. Thus, selling anything would have been challenging, but selling *encyclopedias*, which were about as popular in Hawaii as mosquitoes and mainlanders, was an ordeal. No matter how deftly or forcefully I managed to deliver the key phrases drilled into us during our brief training session ("Boys, tell the folks you ain't selling encyclopedias—you're selling a Vast Compendium of Human Knowledge . . . the Answers to Life's Questions!"), I always got the same response.

Beat it, kid.

If my shyness made me bad at selling encyclopedias, my nature made me despise it. I wasn't built for heavy doses of rejection. I'd known this about myself since high school, freshman year, when I got cut from the baseball team. A small setback, in the grand scheme, but it knocked me sideways. It was my first real awareness that not everyone in this world will like us, or accept us, that we're often cast aside at the very moment we most need to be included.

I will never forget that day. Dragging my bat along the sidewalk, I staggered home and holed up in my room, where I grieved, and moped, for about two weeks, until my mother appeared on the edge of my bed and said, "Enough." She urged me to try something else.

"Like what?" I groaned into my pillow.

"How about track?" she said.

"Track?" I said.

"You can run fast, Buck."

"I can?" I said, sitting up.

So I went out for track. And I found that I *could* run. And no one could take that away.

Now I gave up selling encyclopedias, and all the old familiar

21

rejection that went with it, and I turned to the want ads. In no time I spotted a small ad inside a thick black border in the newspaper. WANTED: SECURITIES SALESMEN. I certainly figured to have better luck selling securities. After all, I had an MBA. And before leaving home I'd had a pretty successful interview with Dean Witter.

I did some research and found that this job had two things going for it. First, it was with Investors Overseas Services, which was headed by Bernard Cornfeld, one of the most famous businessmen of the 1960s. Second, it was located on the top floor of a beautiful beachside tower. Twenty-foot windows overlooking that turquoise sea. Both of these things appealed to me and made me press hard in the interview. Somehow, after weeks of being unable to talk anyone into buying an encyclopedia, I talked Team Cornfeld into taking a flier on me.

Cornfeld's extraordinary success, plus that breathtaking view, made it possible most days to forget that the firm was nothing more than a boiler room. Cornfeld was notorious for asking his employees if they *sincerely* wanted to be rich, and every day a dozen wolfish young men demonstrated that they did, they *sincerely* did. With ferocity, with abandon, they crashed the phones, cold-calling prospects, scrambling desperately to arrange face-to-face meetings. I wasn't a smooth talker. I wasn't any kind of talker. Still, I knew numbers, and I knew the product: Dreyfus Funds. More, I knew how to speak the truth. People seemed to like that. I was quickly able to schedule a few meetings and to close a few sales. Inside a week I'd earned enough in commissions to pay my half of the rent for the next six months, with plenty left over for surfboard wax.

My sense of carpe diem was heightened by the fact that the world was coming to an end. A nuclear standoff with the Soviets had been building for weeks. The Soviets had three dozen missiles in Cuba, the United States wanted them out, and both sides had made their final offer. Negotiations were over and World War III was set to begin any minute. According to the newspapers, missiles would fall from the sky later today. Tomorrow at the latest. The world was Pompeii, and the volcano was already spitting ash. Ah well, everyone agreed, when humanity ends, this will be as good a place as any to watch the rising mushroom clouds. Aloha, civilization.

And then, surprise, the world was spared. The crisis passed. The sky seemed to sigh with relief as the air turned suddenly crisper, calmer. A perfect Hawaiian autumn followed. Days of contentment and something close to bliss.

Followed by a sharp restlessness. One night I turned to Carter. "I think maybe the time has come to leave Shangri-La," I said.

I didn't make a hard pitch. I didn't think I had to. It was clearly time to get back to The Plan. But Carter frowned and stroked his chin. "Gee, Buck, I don't know."

23

He'd met a girl. He wanted to stick around, and how could I argue?

I told him I understood. But I was cast low. I went for a long walk on the beach. Game over, I told myself.

The last thing I wanted was to pack up and return to Oregon. But I couldn't see traveling around the world alone, either. Go home, a faint inner voice told me. Get a normal job. Be a normal person.

Then I heard another faint voice, equally emphatic. No, don't go home. Keep going. Don't stop.

The next day I gave my two weeks' notice at the boiler room. "Too bad, Buck," one of the bosses said, "you had a real future as a salesman."

"God forbid," I muttered.

That afternoon, at a travel agency down the block, I purchased an open plane ticket, good for one year on any airline going anywhere. A sort of Eurail Pass in the sky. On Thanksgiving Day, 1962, I hoisted my backpack and shook Carter's hand.

The captain addressed the passengers in rapid-fire Japanese, and I started to sweat. I looked out the window at the blazing red circle on the wing.

Was my idea crazy? Maybe I was, *in fact*, crazy.

If so, it was too late to seek professional help. The plane

was screeching down the runway, roaring above Hawaii's cornstarch beaches. I looked down at the massive volcanoes growing smaller and smaller. No turning back.

Since it was Thanksgiving, the in-flight meal was turkey, stuffing, and cranberry sauce. Since we were bound for Japan, there was also raw tuna and miso soup. I ate it all while reading the paperbacks I'd stuffed into my backpack. *The Catcher in the Rye* and *Naked Lunch*. I identified with Holden Caulfield, the teenage introvert seeking his place in the world, but Burroughs went right over my head. *The junk merchant doesn't sell his product to the consumer, he sells the consumer to his product.*

Too rich for my blood. I fell asleep. When I woke we were in a steep, rapid descent. Below us lay a startlingly bright Tokyo. The Ginza in particular was like a Christmas tree.

Driving to my hotel, however, I saw only darkness. Vast sections of the city were total liquid black. "War," the cabdriver said. "Many building still bomb." For long, solemn stretches the cabdriver and I said nothing. There was nothing to say.

Finally the driver stopped at the address written in my notebook. A dingy hostel. Beyond dingy. I'd made the reservation through American Express, sight unseen, a mistake, I now realized. I crossed the pitted sidewalk and entered a building that seemed about to implode.

An old Japanese woman behind the front desk bowed to me. I realized she wasn't bowing, she was bent by age, like a tree that's weathered many storms. Slowly she led me to my room, which was more a box. Tatami mat, lopsided table, nothing else. I didn't care. I barely noticed that the tatami mat was wafer thin. I bowed to the bent old woman, bidding her good night. *Oyasumi nasai.* I curled up on the mat and passed out.

Hours later I woke in a room flooded with light. I crawled to the window. Apparently I was in some kind of industrial district on the city's fringe, filled with docks and factories. Everywhere I looked was desolation. Buildings cracked and broken. Block after block simply leveled. Gone.

Luckily my father knew people in Tokyo, including a group of American guys working at United Press International. I took a cab there and the guys greeted me like family. They gave me coffee and a breakfast ring and when I told them where I'd spent the night they laughed. They booked me into a clean, decent hotel. Then they wrote down the names of several good places to eat.

What in God's name are you doing in Tokyo? I explained that I was going around the world. Then I mentioned my Crazy Idea. "Huh," they said, giving a little eye roll. They mentioned two ex-servicemen who ran a monthly magazine called *Importer.* "Talk to the fellas at *Importer,*" they said, "before you do anything rash."

I promised I would. But first, I wanted to see the city.

Guidebook and Minolta box camera in hand, I sought out the few landmarks that had survived the war, the oldest temples and shrines. I spent hours sitting on benches in walled gardens, reading about Japan's dominant religions, Buddhism and Shinto. I marveled at the concept of *kensho*, or satori—enlightenment that comes in a flash, a blinding pop. Sort of like the bulb on my Minolta. I liked that. I wanted that.

But first, I'd need to change my whole approach. I was a linear thinker, and according to Zen, linear thinking is nothing but a delusion, one of the many that keep us unhappy. Reality is nonlinear, Zen says. No future, no past. All is now.

In every religion, it seemed, self is the obstacle, the enemy. And yet Zen declares plainly that the self doesn't exist. Self is a mirage, a fever dream, and our stubborn belief in its reality not only wastes life, but shortens it. Self is the bald-faced lie we tell ourselves daily, and happiness requires seeing through the lie, debunking it. *To study the self*, said the thirteenth-century Zen master Dōgen, *is to forget the self*. Inner voice, outer voices, it's all the same. No dividing lines.

Especially in competition. Victory, Zen says, comes when we forget the self and the opponent, who are but two halves of one whole. In *Zen and the Art of Archery*, it's all laid out with crystal clarity. *Perfection in the art of swordsmanship is reached . . . when the heart is troubled by no more thought of I and You, of the opponent and his sword, of one's own sword and*

27

*how to wield it. . . . All is emptiness: your own self, the flashing
sword, and the arms that wield it. Even the thought of emptiness
is no longer there.*

My head swimming, I decided to take a break, to visit a
very unZen landmark, in fact the most anti-Zen place in Japan,
an enclave where men focused on self and nothing but self—
the Tokyo Stock Exchange. Housed in a marble Romanesque
building with great big Greek columns, the Tosho looked from
across the street like a stodgy bank in a quiet town in Kan-
sas. Inside, however, all was bedlam. Hundreds of men waving
their arms, pulling their hair, screaming. A more depraved version of Cornfeld's boiler room.

I couldn't look away. I watched and watched, asking myself,
Is this what it's all about? Really? I appreciated money as much
as the next guy. But I wanted my life to be about so much more.

After the Tosho I needed peace. I went deep into the
silent heart of the city, to the garden of the nineteenth-
century emperor Meiji and his empress, a space thought to
possess immense spiritual power. I sat, contemplative, rev-
erent, beneath swaying ginkgo trees, beside a beautiful torii
gate. I read in my guidebook that a torii gate is usually a por-
tal to sacred places, and so I basked in the serenity, trying to
soak it all in.

The next morning I laced up my running shoes and jogged
to Tsukiji, the world's largest fish market. It was the Tosho all

over again, with shrimp instead of stocks. I watched ancient fishermen spread their catches onto wooden carts and haggle with leather-faced merchants. That night I took a bus up to the lakes region, in the northern Hakone Mountains, an area that inspired many of the great Zen poets. *You cannot travel the path until you have become the path yourself,* said the Buddha, and I stood in awe before a path that twisted from the glassy lakes to cloud-ringed Mount Fuji, a perfect snow-clad triangle that looked to me exactly like Mount Hood back home. The Japanese believe climbing Fuji is a mystical experience, a ritual act of celebration, and I was overcome with a desire to climb it, right then. I wanted to ascend into the clouds. I decided to wait, however. I would return when I had something to celebrate.

I went back to Tokyo and presented myself at the *Importer* magazine. The two ex-servicemen in charge, thick-necked, brawny, very busy, looked as if they might chew me out for intruding and wasting their time. But within minutes their gruff exterior dissolved and they were warm, friendly, pleased to meet someone from back home. We talked mostly about sports. Can you believe the Yankees won it all again? How about that Willie Mays? None better. Yessir, none better.

Then they told me their story.

They were the first Americans I ever met who loved Japan. Stationed there during the Occupation, they fell under the spell of the culture, and when their hitch was up they simply couldn't bring themselves to leave. So they'd launched an import magazine, when no one anywhere was interested in importing anything Japanese, and somehow they'd managed to keep it afloat for seventeen years.

I told them my Crazy Idea and they listened with some interest. They made a pot of coffee and invited me to sit down. Was there a particular line of Japanese shoes I'd considered importing? they asked. I told them I liked Tiger, a nifty brand manufactured by Onitsuka Co., down in Kobe, the largest city in southern Japan. "Yes, yes, we've seen it," they said.

I told them I was thinking of heading down there, meeting the Onitsuka people face-to-face.

In that case, the men said, you'd better learn a few things about doing business with the Japanese.

"The key," they said, "is don't be pushy. Don't come on like the typical American, the typical gaijin—rude, loud, aggressive, not taking no for an answer. The Japanese do not react well to the hard sell. Negotiations here tend to be soft. It's a culture of indirection. No one ever turns you down flat. No one ever says, straight out, no. But they don't say yes, either. They speak in circles, sentences with no clear subject or object. Don't be discouraged, but don't be cocky. You might leave a man's office thinking you've blown it, when in fact he's ready to do a deal. You might leave thinking you've closed a deal, when in fact you've just been rejected. *You never know.*"

I frowned. Under the best of circumstances I was not a great negotiator. Now I was going to have to negotiate in some kind of funhouse with trick mirrors? Where normal rules didn't apply?

After an hour of this baffling tutorial, I shook hands and said my good-byes. Feeling suddenly that I couldn't wait, while their words were fresh in my mind, I raced back to my hotel, threw everything into my little suitcase and backpack, and phoned Onitsuka to make an appointment.

Later that afternoon I boarded a train south.

Japan was renowned for its impeccable order and extreme cleanliness. Japanese literature, philosophy, clothing, domestic life, all were marvelously pure and spare. Minimalist. *Expect nothing, seek nothing, grasp nothing*—the immortal Japanese poets wrote lines that seemed polished and polished until they gleamed like the blade of a samurai's sword, or the stones of a mountain brook.

So why, I wondered, is this train to Kobe so filthy?

The floors were strewn with newspapers and cigarette butts. The seats were covered with orange rinds and discarded newspapers. Worse, every car was packed. There was barely room to stand.

I found a strap by a window and hung there for seven hours as the train rocked and inched past remote villages, past farms no bigger than the average Portland backyard. The trip was long, but neither my legs nor my patience gave out. I was too busy going over and over my tutorial.

When I arrived I took a small room in a cheap *ryokan*. My appointment at Onitsuka was early the next morning, so I lay down immediately on the tatami mat. But I was too excited to sleep. I rolled around on the mat most of the night, and at dawn I rose wearily and stared at my gaunt, bleary reflection in the mirror. After shaving, I put on my green Brooks Brothers suit and gave myself a pep talk.

You are capable. You are confident. You can do this.

You can DO this.

Then I went to the wrong place.

I presented myself at the Onitsuka showroom, when in fact I was expected at the Onitsuka *factory*—across town. I hailed a taxi and raced there, frantic, arriving half an hour late. Unfazed, a group of four executives met me in the lobby. They bowed. I bowed. One stepped forward. He said his name was Ken Miyazaki, and he wished to give me a tour.

The first shoe factory I'd ever seen. I found everything about it interesting. Even musical. Each time a shoe was molded, the metal last would fall to the floor with a silvery tinkle, a melodic CLING-*clong*. Every few seconds, CLING-*clong*, CLING-*clong*, a cobbler's concerto. The executives seemed to enjoy it, too. They smiled at me and each other.

We passed through the accounting department. Everyone in the room, men and women, leaped from their chairs, and in unison bowed, a gesture of *kei*, respect for the American tycoon. I'd read that "tycoon" came from *taikun*, Japanese for "warlord." I didn't know how to acknowledge their *kei*. To bow or not bow, that is always the question in Japan. I gave a weak smile and a half bow, and kept moving.

The executives told me that they churned out fifteen thousand pairs of shoes each month. "Impressive," I said, not knowing if that was a lot or a little.

They led me into a conference room and pointed me to the chair at the head of a long round table. "Mr. Knight," someone said, "*here*."

Seat of honor. More *kei*. They arranged themselves around the table and straightened their ties and gazed at me. The moment of truth had arrived.

I'd rehearsed this scene in my head so many times, as I'd rehearsed every race I'd ever run, long before the starting pistol. But now I realized this was no race. There is a primal urge to compare everything—life, business, adventures of all sorts—to a race. But the metaphor is often inadequate. It can take you only so far.

Unable to remember what I'd wanted to say, or even why I was here, I took several quick breaths. Everything depended on my rising to this occasion. Everything. If I didn't, if I muffed this, I'd be doomed to spend the rest of my days selling encyclopedias, or mutual funds, or some other junk I didn't really care about. I'd be a disappointment to my parents, my school, my hometown. Myself.

I looked at the faces around the table. Whenever I'd imagined this scene, I'd omitted one crucial element. I'd failed to foresee how present World War II would be in that room. The war was right *there*, beside us, between us, attaching a subtext to every word we spoke.

And yet it also *wasn't* there. The Japanese had put the war cleanly behind them. Also, these executives in the conference room were young, like me, and you could see that they felt the war had nothing to do with them.

On the other hand, the past was past.

On the other hand, that whole question of Winning and Losing, which clouds and complicates so many deals, gets even more complicated when the potential winners and losers have recently been involved, albeit via proxies and ancestors, in a global conflagration.

All of this interior static, this seesawing confusion about war and peace, created a low-volume hum in my head, an awkwardness for which I was unprepared. The realist in me wanted to acknowledge it, the idealist in me pushed it aside. I coughed into my fist. "Gentlemen," I began.

Mr. Miyazaki interrupted. "Mr. Knight, what company are you with?" he asked.

"Ah, yes, good question."

Adrenaline surging through my blood, I felt the flight response, the longing to run and hide, which made me think of the safest place in the world. My parents' house. The house had been built decades before, by people with much more money than my parents, and thus the architect had included servants' quarters at the back of the house, and these quarters were my bedroom, which I'd filled with baseball cards, record albums, posters, books. I'd also covered one wall with my blue ribbons from track, the one thing in my life of which I was unabashedly proud. And so? "Blue Ribbon," I blurted. "Gentlemen, I represent Blue Ribbon Sports of Portland, Oregon."

Mr. Miyazaki smiled. The other executives smiled. A murmur went around the table. *Blueribbon, blueribbon, blueribbon.* The executives folded their hands and fell silent again and resumed staring at me. "Well," I began again, "gentlemen, the American shoe market is enormous. And largely untapped. If Onitsuka can penetrate that market, if Onitsuka can get its Tigers into American stores, and price them to undercut Adidas, which most American athletes now wear, it could be a hugely profitable venture."

I was simply quoting my presentation at Stanford, verbatim, speaking lines and numbers I'd spent weeks and weeks researching and memorizing, and this helped to create an illusion of eloquence. I could see that the executives were impressed. But when I reached the end of my pitch there was a prickling silence. Then one man broke the silence, and then another, and now they were all speaking over one another in loud, excited voices. Not to me, but to each other.

Then, abruptly, they all stood and left.

Was this the customary Japanese way of rejecting a Crazy Idea? To stand in unison and leave? Had I squandered my *kei*—just like that? Was I dismissed? What should I do? Should I just . . . leave?

After a few minutes they returned. They were carrying sketches, samples, which Mr. Miyazaki helped to spread before me. "Mr. Knight," he said, "we've been thinking long time about American market."

"You have?"

"We already sell wrestling shoe in United States. In, eh, Northeast? But we discuss many time bringing other lines to other places in America."

They showed me three different models of Tigers. A training shoe, which they called a Limber Up. "Nice," I said. A high-jump shoe, which they called a Spring Up. "Lovely," I said. And a discus shoe, which they called a Throw Up.

Do not laugh, I told myself. Do not . . . laugh.

They barraged me with questions about the United States, about American culture and consumer trends, about different kinds of athletic shoes available in American sporting goods stores. They asked me how big I thought the American shoe market was, how big it could be, and I told them that ultimately it could be $1 billion. To this day I'm not sure where that number came from. They leaned back, gazed at each other, astonished. Now, to my astonishment, they began pitching me. "Would Blue Ribbon . . . be interested . . . in representing Tiger shoes? In the United States?"

"Yes," I said. "Yes, it *would*."

I held forth the Limber Up. "This is a good shoe," I said. "This shoe—I can sell this shoe." I asked them to ship me samples right away. I gave them my address and promised to send them a money order for fifty dollars.

They stood. They bowed deeply. I bowed deeply. We shook hands. I bowed again. They bowed again. We all smiled. We were partners. We were brothers. The meeting, which I'd expected to last fifteen minutes, had gone two hours.

From Onitsuka I went straight to the nearest American Express office and sent a letter to my father. *Dear Dad: Urgent. Please wire fifty dollars right away to Onitsuka Co. of Kobe.*

Ho ho, hee hee . . . strange things are happening.

Back in my hotel I walked in circles around my tatami mat, trying to decide. Part of me wanted to race back to Oregon, wait for those samples, get a jump on my new business venture.

Also, I was crazed with loneliness, cut off from everything

and everyone I knew. The occasional sight of a *New York Times* or a *Time* magazine gave me a lump in my throat. I was a castaway, a kind of modern Crusoe. I wanted to be home again. Now.

And yet. I was still aflame with curiosity about the world. I still wanted to see, to explore.

Curiosity won.

I went to Hong Kong and walked the mad, chaotic streets, horrified by the sight of legless, armless beggars, old men kneeling in filth, alongside pleading orphans. The old men were mute, but the children had a cry they repeated: *Hey, rich man, hey, rich man, hey, rich man.* Then they'd weep or slap the ground. Even after I gave them all the money in my pockets, the cry never stopped.

I went to the edge of the city, climbed to the top of Victoria Peak, gazed off into the distance at China. In college I'd read the analects of Confucius—*The man who moves a mountain begins by carrying away small stones*—and now I felt strongly that I'd never have a chance to move this particular mountain. I'd never get any closer to that walled-off mystical land, and it made me feel unaccountably sad. Incomplete.

I went to the Philippines, which had all the madness and chaos of Hong Kong, and twice the poverty. I moved slowly, as if in a nightmare, through Manila, through endless crowds and fathomless gridlock.

I went to Bangkok, where I rode a long pole boat through murky swamps to an open-air market that seemed a Thai version of a Hieronymous Bosch painting. I ate birds, and fruits, and vegetables I'd never seen before, and never would again. I dodged rickshaws, scooters, *tuk-tuks*, and elephants to reach Wat Phra Kaew, and one of the most sacred statues in Asia, an enormous six-hundred-year-old Buddha carved from a single hunk of jade. Standing before its placid face, I asked, *Why am I here? What is my purpose?*

I waited.

Nothing.

Or else the silence was my answer.

I went to Vietnam, where streets were bristling with American soldiers, and thrumming with fear. Everyone knew that war was coming. Days before Christmas, 1962, I went on to Calcutta, and rented a room the size of a coffin. No bed, no chair; there wasn't enough space. Just a hammock suspended above a fizzing hole—the toilet. Within hours I fell ill. An airborne virus, probably, or food poisoning. For one whole day I believed that I wouldn't make it. I knew that I was going to die.

But I rallied, somehow, forced myself out of that hammock, and the next day I was walking unsteadily with thousands of pilgrims and dozens of sacred monkeys down the steep staircase of Varanasi temple. The steps led directly into the hot seething Ganges. When the water was at my waist I looked up—a mirage? No, a funeral, taking place in the middle of the river. In fact, several funerals. I watched mourners wade out into the current and place their loved ones atop tall wooden biers, then set them afire. Not twenty yards away, others were calmly bathing. Still others were slaking their thirst with the same water.

The Upanishads say, *Lead me from the unreal to the real.* So I fled the unreal. I flew to Kathmandu and hiked straight up the clean white wall of the Himalayas. On the descent I stopped at a crowded *chowk* and devoured a bowl of buffalo meat, blood rare. The Tibetans in the *chowk*, I noted, wore boots of red wool and green flannel, with upturned wooden toes, not unlike the runners on sleds. Suddenly I was *noticing* everyone's shoes.

I went back to India, spent New Year's Eve wandering the streets of Bombay, weaving in and out among oxen and long-horned cows, feeling the start of an epic migraine—the noise and the smells, the colors and the glare. I went on to Kenya, and took a long bus ride deep into the bush. Giant ostriches tried to outrun the bus, and storks the size of pit bulls floated just outside the windows. Every time the driver stopped, in the middle of nowhere, to pick up a few Maasai warriors, a baboon or two would try to board. The driver and warriors would then chase the baboons off with machetes. Before stepping off the bus, the baboons would always glance over their shoulders and give me a look of wounded pride. Sorry, old man, I thought. If it were up to me.

I went to Cairo, to the Giza plateau, and stood beside desert nomads and their silk-draped camels at the foot of the Great Sphinx, all of us squinting up into its eternally open eyes. The sun hammered down on my head, the same sun that hammered down on the thousands of men who built these pyramids, and the millions of visitors who came after. Not one of them was remembered, I thought. *All is vanity*, says the Bible. *All is now*, says Zen. *All is dust*, says the desert.

I went to Jerusalem, to the rock where Abraham prepared to kill his son, where Muhammad began his heavenward ascent. The Koran says the rock wanted to join Muhammad, and tried to follow, but Muhammad pressed his foot to the rock and stopped it. His footprint is said to be still visible. Was he barefoot or wearing a shoe? I ate a terrible midday meal in a dark tavern, surrounded by soot-faced laborers. Each looked bone-tired. They chewed slowly, absently, like zombies. Why must we work so hard? I thought. *Consider the lilies of the field . . . they neither toil nor spin.* And yet the first-century rabbi Eleazar ben Azariah said our work is the holiest part of us. *All are proud of their craft. God speaks of his work; how much more should man.*

I went on to Istanbul, got wired on Turkish coffee, got lost on the twisty streets beside the Bosphorus. I stopped to sketch the glowing minarets, and toured the golden labyrinths of Topkapi Palace, home of the Ottoman sultans, where Muhammad's sword is now kept. *Don't go to sleep one night,* wrote Rūmī, the thirteenth-century Persian poet. *What you most want will come to you then.*

Warmed by a sun inside you'll see wonders.

I went to Rome, spent days hiding in small trattorias, scarfing mountains of pasta, gazing upon the most beautiful women, and shoes, I'd ever seen. (Romans in the age of the Caesars believed that putting on the right shoe before the left brought prosperity and good luck.) I explored the grassy ruins of Nero's bedroom, the gorgeous rubble of the Coliseum, the vast halls and rooms of the Vatican. Expecting crowds, I was always out the door at dawn, determined to be first in line. But there was never a line. The city was mired in a historic cold snap. I had it all to myself.

Even the Sistine Chapel. Alone under Michelangelo's ceiling, I was able to wallow in my disbelief. I read in my guidebook that Michelangelo was miserable while painting his masterpiece. His back and neck ached. Paint fell constantly into his hair and eyes.

He couldn't wait to be finished, he told friends. If even Michelangelo didn't like his work, I thought, what hope is there for the rest of us?

I went to Florence, spent days seeking Dante, reading Dante,

the angry, exiled misanthrope. Did the misanthropy come first—
or after? Was it the cause or the effect of his anger and exile?

I stood before Michelangelo's *David*, shocked at the anger
in his eyes. Goliath never had a chance.

I went by train up to Milan, communed with Da Vinci,
considered his beautiful notebooks, and wondered at his peculiar obsessions. Chief among them, the human foot. *Masterpiece of engineering*, he called it. *A work of art.*

Who was I to argue?

On my last night in Milan I attended the opera at La
Scala. I aired out my Brooks Brothers suit and wore it proudly
amid the *uomini* poured into custom-tailored tuxedoes and the
donne molded into bejeweled gowns. We all listened in wonder to *Turandot*. As Calaf sang "Nessun dorma"—*Set, stars! At
dawn I will win, I will win, I will win!*—my eyes welled, and
with the fall of the curtain I leaped to my feet. *Bravissimo!*

I went to Venice, spent a few languorous days walking in
the footsteps of Marco Polo, and stood I don't know how long
before the palazzo of Robert Browning. *If you get simple beauty
and naught else, you get about the best thing God invents.*

My time was running out. Home was calling to me. I hurried to Paris, descended far belowground to the Panthéon, put
my hand lightly on the crypts of Rousseau—and Voltaire. *Love
truth, but pardon error.* I took a room in a seedy hotel, watched
sheets of winter rain sluice the alley below my window, prayed

at Notre Dame, got lost in the Louvre. I bought a few books at Shakespeare and Company, and I stood in the spot where Joyce slept, and F. Scott Fitzgerald. I then walked slowly down the Seine, stopping to sip a cappuccino at the café where Hemingway and Dos Passos read the New Testament aloud to each other. On my last day I sauntered up the Champs-Élysées, tracing the liberators' path, thinking all the while of Patton. *Don't tell people how to do things, tell them what to do and let them surprise you with their results.*

Of all the great generals, he was the most shoe-obsessed: *A soldier in shoes is only a soldier. But in boots he becomes a warrior.*

I flew to Munich, visited Bürgerbräukeller, where Hitler fired a gun into the ceiling and started the beginning of what led to World War II. I tried to visit Dachau, but when I asked for directions people looked away, professing not to know. I went to Berlin and presented myself at Checkpoint Charlie. Russian guards in heavy topcoats examined my passport, patted me down, asked what business I had in communist East Berlin. "None," I said. I was terrified that they'd somehow find out I'd attended Stanford. Just before I arrived two Stanford students had tried to smuggle a teenager out in a Volkswagen. They were still in prison.

But the guards waved me through. I walked a little ways and stopped at the corner of Marx-Engels-Platz. I looked around, all directions. Nothing. No trees, no stores, no life. I thought of all the poverty I'd seen in every corner of Asia. This was a different kind of poverty, more willful, somehow, more preventable. I saw three children playing in the street. I walked over, took their picture. Two boys and a girl, eight years old. The girl—red wool hat, pink coat—smiled directly at me. Will I ever forget her? Or her shoes? They were made of cardboard. I went to Vienna, that momentous, coffee-scented crossroads, where Stalin and Trotsky and Tito and Hitler and Jung and Freud all lived, at the same historical moment, and all loitered in the same steamy cafés, plotting how to save (or end) the world. I walked the cobblestones Mozart walked, crossed his graceful Danube on the most beautiful stone bridge I ever saw, stopped before the towering spires of St. Stephen's Church, where Beethoven discovered he was deaf. He looked up, saw birds fluttering from the bell tower, and to his horror . . . he did not hear the bells.

At last I flew to London. I went quickly to Buckingham Palace, Speakers' Corner, Harrods. I granted myself a bit of extra time at Commons. Eyes closed, I conjured the great Churchill. *You ask, What is our aim? I can answer in one word. It is victory, victory at all costs, victory in spite of all terror, victory . . . without victory, there is no survival.* I wanted desperately to hop a bus to Stratford, to see Shakespeare's house. But I was out of time.

I spent my last night thinking back over my trip, making notes in my journal. I asked myself, What was the highlight?

Greece, I thought. No question. Greece.

When I first left Oregon I was most excited about two things on my itinerary.

I wanted to pitch the Japanese my Crazy Idea. And I wanted to stand before the Acropolis.

Hours before boarding my flight at Heathrow, I meditated on that moment, looking up at those astonishing columns, experiencing that bracing shock, the kind you receive from all great beauty, but mixed with a powerful sense of—recognition?

Was it only my imagination? After all, I was standing at the birthplace of Western civilization. Maybe I merely *wanted* it to be familiar. But I didn't think so. I had the clearest thought: I've been here before.

Then, walking up those bleached steps, another thought: This is where it all begins.

On my left was the Parthenon, which Plato had watched the teams of architects and workmen build. On my right was the Temple of Athena Nike. Twenty-five centuries ago, per my guidebook, it had housed a beautiful frieze of the goddess Athena, thought to be the bringer of "nike," or victory.

It was one of many blessings Athena bestowed. She also rewarded the dealmakers. In the *Oresteia* she says: "I admire . . . the eyes of persuasion." She was, in a sense, the patron saint of negotiators.

I don't know how long I stood there, absorbing the energy and power of that epochal place. An hour? Three? I don't know how long after that day I discovered the Aristophanes play, set in the Temple of Nike, in which the warrior gives the king a gift—a pair of new shoes. I don't know when I figured out that the play was called *Knights*. I do know that as I turned to leave I noticed the temple's marble façade. Greek artisans had decorated it with several haunting carvings, including the most famous, in which the goddess inexplicably leans down . . . to adjust the strap of her shoe.

February 24, 1963. My twenty-fifth birthday. I walked through the door on Claybourne Street, hair to my shoulders, beard three inches long. My mother let out a cry. My sisters blinked as if they didn't recognize me, or else hadn't realized I'd been gone. Hugs, shouts, bursts of laughter. My mother made me sit, poured me a cup of coffee. She wanted to hear everything. But I was exhausted. I set my suitcase and backpack in the hall and went to my room. I stared blearily at my blue ribbons. Mr. Knight, what is the name of your company?

I curled up on the bed and sleep came on.

An hour later I woke to my mother calling out, "Dinner!"

My father was home from work, and he embraced me as I came into the dining room. He, too, wanted to hear every detail. And I wanted to tell him.

But first, I wanted to know one thing. "Dad," I said. "Did my shoes come?"

1963

My father invited all the neigbors over for coffee and cake and a special viewing of "Buck's pictures." Dutifully, I stood at the slide projector, savoring the darkness, listlessly clicking the advance button and describing the Pyramids, the Temple of Nike, but I wasn't there. I was at the Pyramids, I was at the Temple of Nike. I was wondering about my shoes.

Four months after the big meeting at Onitsuka, after I'd connected with those executives, and won them over, or so I thought—and still the shoes hadn't arrived. I fired off a letter. *Dear Sirs, Re our meeting of last fall, have you had a chance to ship the samples . . . ?* Then I took a few days off, to sleep, wash my clothes, catch up with friends.

I got a speedy reply from Onitsuka. *Shoes coming,* the letter said. *In just a little more days.*

I showed the letter to my father. He winced. A little more days?

"Buck," he said, chuckling, "that fifty bucks is long gone."

*　*　*

My new look—castaway hair, caveman beard—was too much for my mother and sisters. I'd catch them staring, frowning. I could hear them thinking: bum. So I shaved. Afterward I stood before the little mirror on my bureau in the servants' quarters and told myself, "It's official. You're back."

And yet I wasn't. There was something about me that would never return.

My mother noticed it before anyone else. Over dinner one night she gave me a long, searching look. "You seem more . . . worldly."

Worldly, I thought. Gosh.

Until the shoes arrived, whether or not the shoes ever arrived, I'd need to find some way to earn cash money. Before my trip I'd had that interview with Dean Witter. Maybe I could go back there. I ran it by my father, watching TV. He stretched out in his vinyl recliner and suggested I first go have a chat with his old friend Don Frisbee, CEO of Pacific Power & Light.

I knew Mr. Frisbee. In college I'd done a summer internship for him. I liked him, and I liked that he'd graduated from Harvard Business School. Also, I marveled that he'd gone on, rather quickly, to become CEO of a New York Stock Exchange company.

I recall that he welcomed me warmly that spring day in

49

1963, that he gave me one of those double-handed handshakes and led me into his office, into a chair across from his desk. He settled into his big high-backed leather throne and raised his eyebrows. "So . . . what's on your mind?"

"Honestly, Mr. Frisbee, I don't know what to do . . . about . . . or with . . . a job . . . or career. . . ." Weakly, I added: "My life."

I said I was thinking of going to Dean Witter. Or else maybe coming back to the electric company. Or else maybe working for some large corporation. The light from Mr. Frisbee's office window glinted off his rimless glasses and into my eyes. Like the sun off the Ganges. "Phil," he said, "those are all bad ideas."

"Sir?"

"I don't think you should do any of those things."

"Oh."

"Everyone, but everyone, changes jobs at least three times. So if you go to work for an investment firm now, you'll eventually leave, and then at your next job you'll have to start all over. If you go work for some big company, son, same deal. No, what you want to do, while you're young, is get your CPA. That, along with your MBA, will put a solid floor under your earnings. Then, when you change jobs, which you will, trust me, at least you'll maintain your salary level. You won't go backward."

That sounded practical. I certainly didn't want to go backward.

I hadn't majored in accounting, however. I needed nine more hours to even qualify to take the exam. So I quickly enrolled in three accounting classes at Portland State. "More school?" my father grumbled.

Worse, the school in question wasn't Stanford or Oregon. It was little Portland State.

After getting my nine hours I worked at an accounting firm, Lybrand, Ross Bros. & Montgomery. It was one of the Big Eight national firms, but its Portland branch office was small. One partner, three junior accountants. Suits me, I thought. Smallness meant the firm would be intimate, conducive to learning.

And it did start out that way. My first assignment was a Beaverton company, Reser's Fine Foods, and as the solo man on the job I got to spend quality time with the CEO, Al Reser, who was just three years older than me. I picked up some important lessons from him and enjoyed my time poring over his books. But I was too overworked to fully enjoy it. The trouble with a small satellite branch within a big accounting firm is the workload. Whenever extra work came rolling in, there was no one to take up the slack. During the busy season, November through April, we found ourselves up to our ears, logging twelve-hour days, six days a week, which didn't leave much time to learn.

Also, we were watched. Closely. Our minutes were

counted, to the second. When President Kennedy was tragically killed on November 22, I asked for the day off. I wanted to sit in front of the TV with the rest of the nation and mourn. My boss, however, shook his head. Work first, mourn second. *Consider the lilies of the field . . . they neither toil nor spin.*

I had two consolations. One was money. I was earning five hundred dollars a month. My other consolation was lunch. Each day at noon I'd walk down the street to the local travel agency and stand like Walter Mitty before the posters in the window. Switzerland. Tahiti. Moscow. Bali. I'd grab a brochure and leaf through it while eating a peanut butter and jelly sandwich on a bench in the park. I'd ask the pigeons: *Can you believe it was only a year ago that I was surfing Waikiki? Eating water buffalo stew after an early morning hike in the Himalayas?*

Are the best moments of my life behind me? Was my trip around the world . . . my peak?

The pigeons were less responsive than the statue at Wat Phra Kaew.

This is how I spent the first months of my twenty-fifth year. Quizzing pigeons. Polishing my car.

Writing letters.

Dear Carter, Did you ever leave Shangri-La? I'm an accountant now and giving some thought to blowing my brains out.

1964

The notice arrived right around Christmas, so I must have driven down to the waterfront warehouse the first week of 1964. I don't recall exactly. I know it was early morning. I can see myself getting there before the clerks unlocked the doors.

I handed them the notice and they went into the back and returned with a large box covered in Japanese writing.

I raced home, scurried down to the basement, ripped open the box. Twelve pairs of shoes, creamy white, with blue stripes down the sides. God, they were beautiful. They were more than beautiful. I'd seen nothing in Florence or Paris that surpassed them. I wanted to put them on marble pedestals or in gilt-edged frames. I held them up to the light, caressed them as sacred objects, the way a writer might treat a new set of notebooks or a baseball player a rack of bats.

Then I sent two pairs to my old track coach at Oregon, Bill Bowerman.

I did so without a second thought, since it was Bowerman who'd first made me think, really *think*, about what people put on their feet. Bowerman was a genius coach, a master motivator, a natural leader of young men, and there was one piece of gear he deemed crucial to their development. Shoes. He was obsessed with how human beings are shod.

In the four years I'd run for him at Oregon, Bowerman was constantly sneaking into our lockers and stealing our footwear. He'd spend days tearing them apart, stitching them back up, then hand them back with some minor modification, which made us either run like deer or bleed. Regardless of the results, he never stopped. He was determined to find new ways of bolstering the instep, cushioning the midsole, building out more room for the forefoot. He always had some new design, some new scheme to make our shoes sleeker, softer, lighter. Especially lighter. One ounce sliced off a pair of shoes, he said, is equivalent to 55 pounds over one mile. He wasn't kidding. His math was solid. You take the average man's stride of six feet, spread it out over a mile (5,280 feet), you get 880 steps. Remove one ounce from each step—that's 55 pounds on the button. Lightness, Bowerman believed, directly translated to less burden, which meant more energy, which meant more speed. And speed equaled winning. Bowerman didn't like to lose. (I got it from him.) Thus, lightness was his constant goal.

"Goal" is putting it kindly. In quest of lightness he was willing to try anything. Animal, vegetable, mineral—any material was eligible if it might improve on the standard shoe leather of the day. That sometimes meant kangaroo skin. Other times, cod. You haven't lived until you've competed against the fastest runners in the world wearing shoes made of cod.

There were four or five of us on the track team who were Bowerman's podiatry guinea pigs, but I was his pet project. Something about my feet spoke to him. Something about my stride. Also, I afforded a wide margin of error. I wasn't the best on the team, not by a long shot, so he could afford to make mistakes on me. With my more talented teammates he didn't dare take undue chances.

As a freshman, as a sophomore, as a junior, I lost count of how many races I ran in flats or spikes modified by Bowerman. By my senior year he was making all my shoes from scratch.

Naturally I believed this new Tiger, this funny little shoe from Japan that had taken more than a full year to reach me, would intrigue my old coach. Of course, it wasn't as light as his cod shoes. But it had potential: The Japanese were promising to improve it. Better yet, it was inexpensive. I knew this would appeal to Bowerman's innate frugality.

Even the shoe's name struck me as something Bowerman might flip for. He usually called his runners "Men of Oregon," but every once in a while he'd exhort us to be "tigers." I can see him pacing the locker room, telling us before a race, "Be *TIGERS* out

there!" (If you weren't a tiger, he'd often call you a "hamburger.")
Now and then, when we complained about our skimpy prerace
meal, he'd growl: "A tiger hunts best when he's hungry."

With any luck, I thought, Coach will order a few pairs of
Tigers for his tigers.

But whether or not he placed an order, impressing Bowerman would be enough. That alone would constitute success for
my fledgling company.

It's possible that everything I did in those days was motivated by some deep yearning to impress, to please, Bowerman.
Besides my father, there was no man whose approval I craved
more, and besides my father there was no man who gave it less
often. Frugality carried over to every part of the coach's makeup.
He weighed and hoarded words of praise, like uncut diamonds.

After you'd won a race, if you were lucky, Bowerman might
say: "Nice race." (In fact, that's precisely what he said to one of
his milers after the young man became one of the very first to
crack the mythical four-minute mark in the United States.)
More likely Bowerman would say nothing. He'd stand before
you in his tweed blazer and ratty sweater-vest, his string tie
blowing in the wind, his battered ball cap pulled low, and nod
once. Maybe stare. Those ice-blue eyes, which missed nothing,
gave nothing. Everyone talked about Bowerman's dashing good
looks, his retro crew cut, his ramrod posture and planed jawline,
but what always got *me* was that gaze of pure violet blue.

It got me on Day One. From the moment I arrived at the University of Oregon, in August 1955, I loved Bowerman. And feared him. And neither of these initial impulses ever went away, they were always there between us. I never stopped loving the man, and I never found a way to shed the old fear. Sometimes the fear was less, sometimes more, sometimes it went right down to my shoes, which he'd probably cobbled with his bare hands. Love and fear—the same binary emotions governed the dynamic between me and my father. I wondered sometimes if it was mere coincidence that Bowerman and my father—both cryptic, both alpha, both inscrutable—were both named Bill.

And yet the two men were driven by different demons. My father, the son of a butcher, was always chasing respectability, whereas Bowerman, whose father had been governor of Oregon, didn't give a darn for respectability. He was also the grandson of legendary pioneers, men and women who'd walked the full length of the Oregon Trail. When they stopped walking they founded a tiny town in eastern Oregon, which they called Fossil. Bowerman spent his early days there, and compulsively returned. Part of his mind was always back in Fossil, which was funny, because there was something distinctly fossilized about him. Hard, brown, ancient, he possessed a blend of grit and integrity and stubbornness that was rare. Today it's all but extinct.

He was a war hero, too. Of course he was. As a major in

the Tenth Mountain Division. The most famous track coach in America, Bowerman never considered himself a track coach. He detested being called "Coach." Given his background, he naturally thought of track as a means to an end. He called himself a "Professor of Competitive Responses," and his job, as he saw it, and often described it, was to get you ready for the struggles and competitions that lay ahead, far beyond Oregon.

Despite this lofty mission, or perhaps because of it, the facilities at Oregon were Spartan. Dank wooden walls, lockers that hadn't been painted in decades. The lockers had no door, just slats to separate your stuff from the next guy's. We hung our clothes on nails. *Rusty* nails. We sometimes ran without socks. Complaining never crossed our minds. We saw our coach as a general, to be obeyed quickly and blindly. In my mind he was Patton with a stopwatch.

That is, when he wasn't a god.

Like all the ancient gods, Bowerman lived on a mountaintop. His ranch sat on a peak high above the campus. And when reposing on his private Olympus, he could be vengeful as the gods.

I remember only one time when he got really sore with me. I was a sophomore, being worn down by my schedule. Class all morning, practice all afternoon, homework all night. One day, fearing that I was coming down with the flu, I stopped by Bowerman's office to say that I wouldn't be able to practice that afternoon. "Uh-huh," he said. "Who's the coach of this team?"

"You are."

"Well, as coach of this team I'm telling you to get out there. And by the way . . . we're going to have a time trial today."

I was close to tears. But I held it together, channeled all my emotion into my run, and posted one of my best times of the year. As I walked off the track I glowered at Bowerman. *Happy now?* He looked at me, checked his stopwatch, looked at me again, nodded. He'd tested me. He'd broken me down and remade me, just like a pair of shoes. And I'd held up. Thereafter, I was truly one of his Men of Oregon. From that day on, I was a tiger.

I heard back right away from Bowerman. He wrote to say he was coming to Portland the following week, for the Oregon Indoor. He invited me to lunch at the Cosmopolitan Hotel, where the team would be staying.

January 25, 1964. I was terribly nervous as the waitress showed us to our table. I recall that Bowerman ordered a hamburger, and I said croakily: "Make it two."

We spent a few minutes catching up. I told Bowerman about my trip around the world. Kobe, Jordan, the Temple of Nike. Bowerman was especially interested in my time in Italy, which, despite his brushes with death, he remembered fondly.

At last he came to the point. "Those Japanese shoes," he said. "They're pretty good. How about letting me in on the deal?"

I looked at him. In? Deal? It took me a moment to absorb and understand what he was saying. He didn't merely want to buy a dozen Tigers for his team, he wanted to become—my partner? Had God spoken from the whirlwind and asked to be my partner, I wouldn't have been more surprised. I stammered, and stuttered, and said yes.

I put out my hand.

But then I pulled it back. "What kind of partnership did you have in mind?" I asked.

I was daring to negotiate with God. I couldn't believe my nerve.

Nor could Bowerman. He looked bemused. "Fifty-fifty," he said. "Well, you'll have to put up half the money."

"Of course."

"I figure the first order will be for a thousand dollars. Your half will be five hundred."

"I'm good for that."

When the waitress dropped off the check for the two hamburgers, we split that, too. Fifty-fifty.

I remember it as the next day, or maybe sometime in the next few days or weeks, and yet all the documents contradict my memory. Letters, diaries, appointment books—they all definitively show it taking place much later. But I remember what I remember, and there must be a reason why I remember it the way I do. As we left the restaurant that day, I can *see* Bowerman putting on his ball cap, I can *see* him straightening his string tie, I can *hear* him saying: "I'll need you to meet my lawyer, John Jaqua. He can help us get this in writing."

Either way, days later, weeks later, years later, the meeting happened like this.

I pulled up to Bowerman's stone fortress and marveled, as I always did, at the setting. Remote. Not many folks made it out there. Along Coburg Road to Mackenzie Drive until you found a winding dirt lane that went a couple miles up the hills into the woods. Eventually you came to a clearing with rose-bushes, solitary trees, and a pleasant house, small but solid, with a stone face. Bowerman had built it with his bare hands. As I slipped my car into park, I wondered how on earth he'd managed all that backbreaking labor by himself. *The man who moves a mountain begins by carrying away small stones.*

Wrapped around the house was a wide wooden porch, with several camp chairs—he'd built that by himself, too. It afforded sweeping views of the McKenzie River, and it wouldn't have taken much convincing to have me believing Bowerman had laid the river between its banks as well.

Now I saw Bowerman standing on the porch. He squinted and strode down the steps toward my car. I don't remember a lot of small talk as he got in. I just slammed it into drive and set a course for his lawyer's house.

Besides being Bowerman's lawyer and best friend, Jaqua was his next-door neighbor. Driving there, I couldn't imagine how this was going to be good for me. I got along fine with Bowerman, sure, and we had ourselves a deal, but lawyers always messed things up. Lawyers specialized in messing things up. And best friend–lawyers . . . ? Bowerman, meanwhile, was doing nothing to put my mind at ease.

Amid the booming silence I kept my eyes on the road and mulled over Bowerman's eccentric personality, which carried over to everything he did. He always went against the grain. Always. For example, he was the first college coach in America to emphasize rest, to place as much value on recovery as on work. But when he worked you, brother, he worked you. Bowerman's strategy for running the mile was simple. Set a fast pace for the first two laps, run the third as hard as you can, then triple your speed on the fourth. There was a Zen-like quality to this strategy, because it was impossible. And yet it worked. Bowerman coached more sub-four-minute milers than anybody, ever. I wasn't one of them, however, and this day I wondered if I was going to fall short once again in that crucial final lap.

We found Jaqua standing out on his porch. I'd met him before, at a track meet or two, but I'd never gotten a really good look at him. Though bespectacled, and sneaking up on middle age, he didn't square with my idea of a lawyer. He was too sturdy, too well made. I learned later that he'd been a star tailback in high school, and one of the best hundred-meter men ever at Pomona College. He still had that telltale athletic power. It came right through his handshake.

The day was typical for Oregon in January. Along with the spitting rain, a deep, wet cold permeated everything. We arranged ourselves on chairs around Jaqua's fireplace, the biggest fireplace I ever saw, big enough to roast an elk. Roaring flames were spinning around several logs the size of hydrants. From a side door came Jaqua's wife carrying a tray. Mugs of hot chocolate. She asked if I'd like whipped cream or marshmallows. "Neither, thank you, ma'am." My voice was two octaves higher than normal. She tilted her head and gave me a pitying look. *Boy, they're going to skin you alive.*

Jaqua took a sip, wiped the cream from his lips, and began. He talked a bit about Oregon track, and about Bowerman. He was wearing dirty blue jeans and a wrinkled flannel shirt, and I couldn't stop thinking how unlawyerly he looked.

Now Jaqua said he'd never seen Bowerman this pumped up about an idea. I liked the sound of that. "But," he added, "fifty-fifty is not so hot for Coach. He doesn't want to be in charge, and he doesn't want to be at loggerheads with you, ever. How about we make it fifty-one–forty-nine? We give you operating control?"

His whole demeanor was that of a man trying to help, to make this situation a win for everyone. I trusted him.

"Fine by me," I said. "That . . . all?"

He nodded. "Deal?" he said.

"Deal," I said.

We all shook hands, signed the papers, and I was now officially in a legal and binding partnership with Almighty Bowerman. Mrs. Jaqua asked if I'd care for more hot chocolate.

"Yes, please, ma'am. And do you have any marshmallows?"

Later that day I wrote Onitsuka and asked if I could be the exclusive distributor of Tiger shoes in the western United States. Then I asked them to send three hundred pairs of Tigers, ASAP. At $3.33 a pair that was roughly $1,000 worth of shoes. Even with Bowerman's kick-in, that was more than I had on hand. Again I put the touch on my father. This time he balked. He didn't mind getting me started, but he didn't want me coming back to him year after year. Besides, he'd thought this shoe thing was a lark. He hadn't sent me to Oregon and Stanford to become a door-to-door shoe salesman, he said.

I looked at my mother. As usual, she said nothing. She simply smiled, vaguely, prettily. I got my shyness from her, that was plain. I often wished I'd also gotten her looks.

The first time my father laid eyes on my mother, he thought she was a mannequin. He was walking by the only department store in Roseburg and there she was, standing in the window, modeling an evening gown. Realizing that she was flesh and blood, he went straight home and begged his sister to find out the name of that gorgeous gal in the window. His sister found out. That's Lota Hatfield, she said.

Eight months later my father proposd and made her Lota Knight.

At the time my father was on his way to becoming an established lawyer, on his way to escaping the terrible poverty that defined his childhood. He was twenty-eight years old. My mother, who had just turned twenty-one, had grown up even poorer than he had. (Her father was a railroad conductor.) Poverty was one of the few things they had in common.

In many ways they were the classic case of opposites attracting. My mother, tall, stunning, a lover of the outdoors, was always seeking places to regain some lost inner peace. My father, small, average, with thick rimless glasses to correct his 20/450 vision, was engaged in a daily, noisome battle to overcome his past, to become respectable, mainly through academics and hard work. Second in his law school class, he never tired of complaining about the one C on his transcript.

When their diametrically opposed personalities caused problems, my parents would fall back on the thing they had most deeply in common: their belief that family comes first. When that consensus didn't work, there were difficult days. And nights.

Her façade could be deceiving, however. Perhaps nothing

ever revealed my mother's true nature like the frequent drills she put me through. She often tied a rope to the post of my bed and made me use it to rappel out of my second-floor window so I would learn what to do in case of fire. While she timed me. What must the neighbors have thought? What must I have thought? Probably this: Life is dangerous. And this: We must always be prepared.

And this: My mother loves me.

When I was twelve, Les Steers and his family moved in across the street, next to my best friend, Jackie Emory. One day Mr. Steers set up a high-jump course in Jackie's backyard, and Jackie and I did battle. Each of us maxed out at four feet six inches. "Maybe one of you will break the world record one day," Mr. Steers said. (I learned later that the world record at that time, six feet eleven inches, belonged to Mr. Steers.)

Out of nowhere my mother appeared. (She was wearing gardening slacks and a summery blouse.) Uh-oh, I thought, we're in trouble. She looked over the scene, looked at me and Jackie. Looked at Mr. Steers. "Move the bar up," she said.

She slipped off her shoes, toed her mark, and burst forward, clearing five feet easily.

I don't know if I ever loved her more.

In the moment I thought she was cool. Soon after, I realized she was also a closet trackophile.

It happened my sophomore year of high school. I developed a painful wart on the bottom of my foot. The podiatrist recommended surgery, which would mean a lost season of track. My mother had two words for that podiatrist. "Un. Acceptable." She marched down to the drugstore and bought a vial of wart remover, which she applied each day to my foot. Then, every two weeks, she took a carving knife and pared away a sliver of the wart, until it was all gone. That spring I posted the best times of my life.

So I shouldn't have been too surprised by my mother's next move when my father reminded me that I needed to get more serious. Casually she opened her purse and took out seven dollars. "I'd like to purchase one pair of Limber Ups, please," she said, loud enough for him to hear.

The sight of her standing at the stove or the kitchen sink, cooking dinner or washing dishes in a pair of Japanese running shoes, size 6, never failed to move me.

Soon thereafter, my father loaned me the thousand bucks. This time the shoes came right away.

April 1964. I rented a truck, drove down to the warehouse district, and the customs clerk handed over ten enormous cartons. Again I hurried home, carried the cartons down to the basement, ripped them open. Each carton held thirty pairs of Tigers, and each pair was wrapped in cellophane. (Shoe boxes would have been too costly.) Within minutes the basement was filled with shoes. I admired them, studied them, played with them, rolled around on top of them. Then I stacked them out of the way, arranging them neatly around the furnace and under the Ping-Pong table, as far as possible from the washer and dryer, so my mother could still do laundry. Lastly, I tried on a pair. I ran circles around the basement. I jumped for joy.

Days later came a letter from Mr. Miyazaki. Yes, he said, *you* can be the distributor for Onitsuka in the West.

That was all I needed. To my father's horror, and my mother's subversive delight, I quit my job at the accounting firm, and all that spring I did nothing but sell shoes out of the trunk of my car.

My sales strategy was simple, and I thought rather brilliant. After being rejected by a couple of sporting goods stores ("Kid, what this world does not need is another track shoe!"), I drove all over the Pacific Northwest, to various track meets. Between races I'd chat up the coaches, the runners, the fans, and show them my wares. The response was always the same. I couldn't write orders fast enough.

Driving back to Portland I'd puzzle over my sudden success at selling. I'd been unable to sell encyclopedias, and I'd despised it to boot. I'd been slightly better at selling mutual funds, but I'd felt dead inside. So why was selling shoes so different? Because, I realized, it wasn't selling. I *believed* in running. I believed that if people got out and ran a few miles every day, the world would be a better place, and I believed these shoes were better to run in. People, sensing my belief, wanted some of that belief for themselves.

Belief, I decided. Belief is irresistible.

Sometimes people wanted my shoes so badly that they'd write me, or phone me, saying they'd heard about the new Tigers and just had to have a pair, could I please send them, collect on delivery? Without my even trying, my mail-order business was born.

Sometimes people would simply show up at my parents' house. Every few nights the doorbell would ring, and my father, grumbling, would get up from his vinyl recliner and turn down the TV and wonder who in the world. There on the porch would be some skinny kid with oddly muscular legs, shifty-eyed and twitchy, like a junky looking to score. "Buck here?" the kid would say. My father would call through the kitchen to my room in the servants' quarters. I'd come out, invite the kid in, show him over to the sofa, then kneel before him and measure his foot. My father, hands jammed into his pockets, would watch the whole transaction, incredulous.

Most people who came to the house had found me through word of mouth. Friend of a friend. But a few found me through my first attempt at advertising—a handout I'd designed and produced at a local print shop. Along the top, in big type, it said: BEST NEWS IN FLATS! JAPAN CHALLENGES EUROPEAN TRACK SHOE DOMINATION! The handout then went on to explain: *Low Japanese labor costs make it possible for an exciting new firm to offer these shoes at the low low price of $6.95.* Along the bottom was my address and phone number. I nailed them up all over Portland.

On July 4, 1964, I sold out my first shipment. I wrote to Tiger and ordered nine hundred more. That would cost roughly three thousand dollars, which would wipe out my father's petty cash, and patience. The Bank of Dad, he said, is now closed. He did agree, grudgingly, to give me a letter of guarantee, which I took down to the First National Bank of Oregon. On the strength of my father's reputation, and nothing more, the bank approved the loan. My father's vaunted respectability was finally paying dividends, at least for me.

I had a venerable partner, a legitimate bank, and a product that was selling itself. I was on a roll.

In fact, the shoes sold so well, I decided to hire another salesman.

Maybe two. In California.

The problem was, how to get to California? I certainly couldn't afford airfare. And I didn't have time to drive. So every other weekend I'd load a duffel bag with Tigers, put on my crispest Army uniform, and head out to the local air base.

Seeing the uniform, the MPs would wave me onto the next military transport to San Francisco or Los Angeles, no questions asked. When I went to Los Angeles I'd save even more money by crashing with Chuck Cale, a friend from Stanford. A good friend. When I'd presented my running-shoe paper to my entrepreneurship class, Cale showed up, for moral support.

During one of those Los Angeles weekends, I attended a meet at Occidental College. As always I stood on the infield grass, letting the shoes do their magic. Suddenly a guy sauntered up and held out his hand. Twinkly eyes, handsome face. In fact, very handsome—though also sad. Despite the enameled calm of his expression, there was something sorrowful, almost tragic, around the eyes. Also, something vaguely familiar.

"Phil," he said.

"Yes?" I said.

"Jeff Johnson," he said.

Of course! Johnson. I'd known him at Stanford. He'd been a runner, a pretty fair miler, and we'd competed against each other at several all-comer meets. And sometimes he'd gone for a run with me and Cale, then for a bite after. "Heya, Jeff," I said, "what are you up to these days?"

"Grad school," he said, "studying anthro." The plan was to become a social worker.

"No kidding," I said, arching an eyebrow. Johnson didn't seem the social worker type. I couldn't see him counseling drug

71

addicts and placing orphans. Nor did he seem the anthropologist type. I couldn't imagine him chatting up cannibals in New Guinea, or scouring Anasazi campsites with a toothbrush, sifting through goat dung for pottery shards.

But these, he said, were merely his daytime drudgeries. On weekends he was following his heart, selling shoes. "No!" I said.

"Adidas," he said.

"Screw Adidas," I said, "you should work for me, help me sell these new Japanese running shoes."

I handed him a Tiger flat, told him about my trip to Japan, my meeting with Onitsuka. He bent the shoe, examined the sole. "Pretty cool," he said. He was intrigued, but no. "I'm getting married," he said. "Not sure I can take on a new venture right now."

I didn't take his rejection to heart. It was the first time I'd heard the word "no" in months.

Life was good. Life was grand. I even had a sort of girlfriend, though I didn't have much time for her. I was happy, maybe as happy as I'd ever been, and happiness can be dangerous. It dulls the senses. Thus, I wasn't prepared for that dreadful letter.

It was from a high school wrestling coach in some benighted town back east, some little burg on Long Island called Valley Stream or Massapequa or Manhasset. I had to read it twice before I understood. The coach claimed that he was just back from Japan, where he'd met with top executives at Onitsuka, who'd anointed him their exclusive American distributor. Since he'd heard that I was selling Tigers, I was therefore poaching, and he ordered me—ordered me!—to stop.

Heart pounding, I phoned my cousin Doug Houser. He'd graduated from Stanford Law School and was now working at a respected firm in town. I asked him to look into this Mr. Manhasset, find out what he could, then back the guy off with a letter. "Saying what, exactly?" Cousin Houser asked.

"That any attempt to interfere with Blue Ribbon will be met with swift legal reprisal," I said.

My "business" was two months old and I was embroiled in a legal battle? Served me right for daring to call myself happy.

Next I sat down and dashed off a frantic letter to Onitsuka. *Dear Sirs, I was very distressed to receive a letter this morning from a man in Manhasset, New York, who claims . . . ?*

I waited for a response. And waited.

I wrote again.

Nanimo.

Nothing.

Cousin Houser found out that Mr. Manhasset was something of a celebrity. Before becoming a high school wrestling coach, he'd been a model—one of the original models for the successful Marlboro Men ad campaign. Horses, hats, landscaped, they worked the whole cowboy thing. Beautiful, I thought. Just what I need. A coast-to-coast match with some mythic American cowboy.

I went into a deep funk. I became such a grouch, such poor company, the girlfriend fell away. Each night I'd sit with my family at dinner, moving my mother's pot roast and vegetables around my plate. Then I'd sit with my father in the nook, staring glumly at the TV. "Buck," my father said, "you look like someone hit you in the back of the head with a two-by-four. Snap out of it."

But I couldn't. I kept going over my meeting at Onitsuka. The executives had shown me such *kei*. They'd bowed to me, and vice versa. I'd been straightforward with them, honest—for the most part. Sure, I hadn't "technically" owned a "business" called Blue Ribbon. But that was splitting hairs. I owned one now, and it had single-handedly brought Tigers to the West Coast, and it could sell Tigers ten times faster if Onitsuka gave me half a chance. Instead, the company was going to cut me out? Throw me over for the East Coast Cowboy?

Toward summer's end I still hadn't heard from Onitsuka, and I'd all but given up on the idea of selling shoes. Labor Day, however, I had a change of heart. I couldn't give up. Not yet. And not giving up meant flying back to Japan. I needed to force a showdown with Onitsuka.

I ran the idea by my father. He still didn't like me fooling around with shoes. But what he really didn't like was someone mistreating his son. He furrowed his brow. "You should probably go," he said.

I talked it over with my mother. "No probablys about it," she said. In fact, she'd drive me to the airport.

Fifty years later I can see us in that car. I can recall every detail. It was a bright, clear day, no humidity, temperature in the low eighties. Both of us, quietly watching the sunlight play across the windshield, said nothing. The silence between us was like the silence on the many days she drove me to meets. I was too busy fighting my nerves to talk, and she, better than anyone, understood. She respected the lines we draw around ourselves in crisis.

Then, as we neared the airport, she broke the silence. "Just be yourself," she said.

I looked out the window. Be myself. Really? Is that my best option? *To study the self is to forget the self.*

I looked down. I certainly wasn't dressed like myself. I was wearing a new suit, a proper charcoal gray, and toting a small suitcase. In the side pocket was a new book: *How to Do Business with the Japanese.* Heaven only knows how or where I'd heard about it. And now I grimace to remember this last detail: I was also wearing a black bowler hat. I'd bought it expressly for this trip, thinking it made me look older. In fact, it made me look mad. Stark, staring mad. As if I'd escaped from a Victorian insane asylum inside a painting by Magritte.

I spent most of the flight memorizing *How to Do Business with the Japanese*. When my eyes grew tired I shut the book and stared out the window. I tried to talk to myself, to coach myself up. I told myself that I needed to put aside hurt feelings, put aside all thoughts of injustice, which would only make me emotional and keep me from thinking clearly. Emotion would be fatal. I needed to remain cool.

I thought back on my running career at Oregon. I'd competed with, and against, men far better, faster, more physically gifted. Many were future Olympians. And yet I'd trained myself to forget this unhappy fact. People reflexively assume that competition is always a good thing, that it always brings out the best in people, but that's only true of people who can forget the competition. The art of competing, I'd learned from track, is the art of forgetting, and I now reminded myself of that fact. You must forget your limits. You must forget your doubts, your pain, your past. You must forget that internal voice screaming, begging, *Not one more step!* And when it's not possible to forget it, you must negotiate with it. I thought over all the races in which my mind wanted one thing, and my body wanted another, those laps in which I'd had to tell my body,

Yes, you raise some excellent points, but let's keep going anyway . . .

Despite all my negotiations with that voice, the skill had never come naturally, and now I feared that I was out of practice. As the plane swooped down toward Haneda Airport I told myself that I'd need to summon the old skill quickly, or lose.

I could not bear the thought of losing.

The 1964 Olympics were about to be held in Japan, so I had my pick of brand-new, reasonably priced lodgings in Kobe. I got a room right downtown, at the Newport, which featured a revolving restaurant on the top. Just like the one atop the Space Needle—a touch of the Great Northwest to settle my nerves. Before unpacking, I phoned Onitsuka and left a message. *I'm here and I request a meeting.*

Then I sat on the edge of the bed and stared at the phone.

At last it rang. A prim-sounding secretary informed me that my contact at Onitsuka, Mr. Miyazaki, no longer worked there. Bad sign. His replacement, Mr. Morimoto, did not wish me to come to the company's headquarters. Very bad sign. Instead, she said, Mr. Morimoto would meet me for tea in my hotel's revolving restaurant. Tomorrow morning.

I went to bed early, slept fitfully. Dreams of car chases, prison, duels—the same dreams that always plagued me the night before a big meet, or date, or exam. I rose at dawn, ate a breakfast of raw egg poured over hot rice, and some grilled fish, and washed it down with a pot of green tea. Then, reciting memorized passages from *How to Do Business with the Japanese*, I shaved my pale jaws. I cut myself once or twice, and had trouble stopping the bleeding. I must have been a sight. Finally I put on my suit and shambled onto the elevator. As I pressed the button for the top floor I noticed that my hand was white as bone. Morimoto arrived on time. He was about my age, but far more mature, more self-assured. He wore a rumpled sport coat and had a kind of rumpled face. We sat at a table by the window. Immediately, before the waiter came to take our order, I launched into my pitch, saying everything I'd vowed not to say. I told Morimoto how distressed I was by this East Coast Cowboy encroaching on my turf. I said I'd been under the impression that I'd made a personal connection with the executives I'd met the previous year, and the impression was underscored by a letter from Mr. Miyazaki saying the thirteen western states were exclusively mine. I was therefore at a loss to explain this treatment. I appealed to Morimoto's sense of fairness, to his sense of honor. He looked uncomfortable, so I took a breath, paused. I raised it from the personal to the professional. I cited my robust sales. I dropped the name of my partner, the legendary coach whose reputation had cachet even on the other side of the Pacific. I emphasized all that I might do for Onitsuka in the future, if given a chance.

Morimoto took a sip of tea. When it was clear that I'd talked myself out, he set down his cup and looked out the window. Slowly we rotated above Kobe. "I will get back to you."

Another fitful night. I got up several times, went to the window, watched the ships bobbing on Kobe's dark purple bay. Beautiful place, I thought. Too bad all beauty is beyond me. The world is without beauty when you lose, and I was about to lose, big-time. I knew that in the morning Morimoto would tell me he was sorry, nothing personal, it was just business, but they were going with the East Coast Cowboy.

At 9:00 a.m. the phone by the bed rang. Morimoto. "Mr. Onitsuka . . . *himself* . . . wishes to see you," he said.

I put on my suit and took a taxi to Onitsuka headquarters. In the conference room, the familiar conference room, Morimoto pointed me to a chair in the middle of the table. The middle this time, not the head. No more *kei*. He sat across from me and stared at me as the room slowly filled with executives. When everyone was there, Morimoto nodded to me. "*Hai*," he said.

I plunged in, essentially repeating what I'd said to him the previous morning. As I built to my crescendo, as I prepared to close, all heads swiveled toward the door, and I stopped midsentence. The temperature of the room dropped ten degrees. The founder of the company, Mr. Onitsuka, had arrived.

Dressed in a dark blue Italian suit, with a head of black hair as thick as shag carpet, he filled every man in the conference room with fear. He seemed oblivious, however. For all his power, for all his wealth, his movements were deferential. He came forward haltingly, with a shuffling gait, giving no sign that he was the boss of all bosses, the shogun of shoes. Slowly he made his way around the table, making brief eye contact with each executive. Eventually he came to me. We bowed to each other, shook hands. Now he took the seat at the head of the table and Morimoto tried to summarize my reason for being there. Mr. Onitsuka raised a hand, cut him off.

Without preamble he launched into a long, passionate monologue. Some time ago, he said, he'd had a vision. A wondrous glimpse of the future. "Everyone in the world wear athletic shoes all the time," he said. "I know this day come." He paused, looking around the table at each person, to see if they also knew. His gaze rested on me. He smiled. I smiled. He blinked twice. "You remind me of myself when I am young," he said softly. He stared into my eyes. One second. Two. Now he turned his gaze to Morimoto. "This about those thirteen western states?" he said.

"Yes," Morimoto said.

"Hm," Onitsuka said. "Hmmmm." He narrowed his eyes, looked down. He seemed to be meditating. Again he looked up at me. "Yes," he said, "all right. You have western states."

The man from New York, he said, could continue selling his wrestling shoes nationwide, but would limit his track shoe sales to the East Coast. Mr. Onitsuka would personally write to him and inform him of this decision.

He rose. I rose. Everyone rose. We all bowed. He left the conference room.

Everyone remaining in the conference room exhaled. "So . . . it is decided," Morimoto said.

For one year, he added. Then the subject would be revisited.

I thanked Morimoto, assured him that Onitsuka wouldn't regret its faith in me. I went around the table shaking everyone's hand, bowing, and when I came back to Morimoto I gave his hand an extra-vigorous shake. I then followed a secretary into a side room, where I signed several contracts, and placed an order for a whopping thirty-five hundred dollars' worth of shoes.

I ran all the way back to my hotel. Halfway there I started skipping, then leaping through the air like a dancer. I stopped at a railing and looked out at the bay. None of its beauty was lost on me now. I watched the boats gliding before a brisk wind and decided that I would hire one. I would take a ride on the Inland Sea. An hour later I was standing in the prow of a boat, wind in my hair, sailing into the sunset and feeling pretty good about myself.

The next day I boarded a train to Tokyo. It was time, at last, to ascend into the clouds.

All the guidebooks said to climb Mount Fuji at night. A proper climb, they said, must culminate with a view of sunrise from the summit. So I arrived at the base of the mountain promptly at dusk. The day had been muggy, but the air was growing cooler, and right away I rethought my decision to wear Bermuda shorts, a T-shirt, and Tigers. I saw a man coming down the mountain in a rubberized coat. I stopped him and offered him three dollars for his coat. He looked at me, looked at the coat, nodded.

I was negotiating successful deals all over Japan!

As night fell hundreds of natives and tourists appeared and began streaming up the mountain. All, I noticed, were carrying long wooden sticks with tinkling bells attached. I spotted an older British couple and asked them about these sticks. "They ward off evil spirits," the woman said.

"There are *evil spirits* on this mountain?" I asked.

"Presumably."

I bought a stick.

I then noticed people gathering at a roadside stand and buying straw shoes. The British woman explained that Fuji was an active volcano, and its ash and soot were guaranteed to ruin shoes. Climbers therefore wore disposable straw sandals.

I bought sandals.

Poorer, but properly outfitted at last, I set off.

There were many ways down Mount Fuji, according to my guidebook, but only one way up. Life lesson in that, I thought. Signs along the upward path, written in many languages, said there would be nine stations before the summit, each offering food and a place to rest. Within two hours, however, I'd passed Station 3 several times. Did the Japanese count differently? Alarmed, I wondered if thirteen western states might actually mean three?

At Station 7, I stopped and bought a Japanese beer and a cup of noodles. While eating my dinner I fell to talking with another couple. They were Americans, younger than me—students, I assumed. He was preppy. Golf slacks and tennis shirt and cloth belt—he was all the colors of an Easter egg. She was pure beatnik. Torn jeans, faded T-shirt, wild dark hair. Her wide-set eyes were brown-black. Like little cups of espresso.

Both were sweating from the climb. They mentioned that I wasn't. I shrugged and said that I'd run track at Oregon. "Half miler."

The young man scowled. His girlfriend said, "Wow." We finished our beers and resumed climbing together.

Her name was Sarah. She was from Maryland. Horse country, she said. Rich country, I thought. She'd grown up riding, and jumping, and showing, and still spent much of her time in saddles and show rings. She talked about her favorite ponies and horses as if they were her closest friends.

I asked about her family. "Daddy owns a candy bar company," she said. She mentioned the company and I laughed. I'd eaten many of her family's candy bars, sometimes before a race. The company was founded by her grandfather, she said, though she hastened to add that she had no interest in money.

I caught her boyfriend scowling again.

She was studying philosophy at Connecticut College for Women. "Not a great school," she said apologetically. She'd wanted to go to Smith, where her sister was a senior, but she didn't get in.

"You sound as if you haven't gotten over the rejection," I said.

"Not even close," she said.

"Rejection is never easy," I said.

"You can say that again."

Her voice was peculiar. She pronounced certain words oddly, and I couldn't decide if it was a Maryland accent or a speech impediment. Whichever, it was adorable.

She asked what brought me to Japan. I explained that I'd come to save my shoe company. "Your *company?*" she said. Clearly she was thinking about the men in her family, founders of companies, captains of industry. Entrepreneurs.

"Yes," I said, "my company."

"And did you . . . save it?" she asked.

"I did," I said.

"All the boys back home are going to business school," she said, "and then they all plan to become *bankers*." She rolled her eyes, adding: "Everyone does the same thing—so boring."

"Boredom scares me," I said.

"Ah. That's because you're a rebel."

I stopped climbing, stabbed my walking stick into the ground.

Me—a rebel? My face grew warm.

As we neared the summit, the path grew narrow. I mentioned that it reminded me of a trail I'd hiked in the Himalayas. Sarah and the boyfriend stared. *Himalayas?* Now she was really impressed. And he was really put out. As the summit came slowly into view, the climb became tricky, treacherous. She seized my hand. "The Japanese have a saying," her boyfriend shouted over his shoulder, to us, to everyone. "A wise man climbs Fuji once. A fool climbs it twice."

No one laughed. Though I wanted to. On the very top we came to a large wooden torii gate. We sat beside it and waited. The air was strange. Not quite dark, not quite light. Then the sun crept above the horizon. I told Sarah and her boyfriend that the Japanese place torii gates at sacral borderlands, portals between this world and the world beyond. "Wherever you pass from the profane to the sacred," I said, "you'll find a torii gate."

Sarah liked that. I told her that Zen masters believed mountains "flow," but that we can't always perceive the flow with our limited senses, and indeed, in that moment, we did feel as if Fuji were flowing, as if we were riding a wave across the world.

Unlike the climb up, the climb down took no effort, and no time. At the bottom I bowed and said good-bye to Sarah and the Easter egg. "*Yoroshiku ne.*" Nice meeting you.

"Where you headed?" Sarah asked.

"I think I'm going to stay at the Hakone Inn tonight," I said.

"Well," she said, "how about we hang out tomorrow?"

I took a step back. I looked at the boyfriend. He scowled. I realized at last that he wasn't her boyfriend. Happy Easter.

We spent two days at the inn, laughing, talking, falling. Beginning. If only this could never end, we said, but of course it had to. I had to go back to Tokyo, to catch a flight home, and Sarah was determined to move on, see the rest of Japan. We made no plans to see each other again. She was a free spirit, she didn't believe in plans. "Good-bye," she said.

"*Hajimemashite,*" I said. Lovely meeting you.

Hours before I boarded my plane, I stopped at the American Express office. I knew she'd have to stop there, too, at some point, to get money from the Candy Bar People. I left her a note: *You've got to fly over Portland to get to the East Coast . . . why not stop for a visit?*

* * *

On my first night home, over dinner, I told my family the good news. I'd met a girl.

Then I told them the other good news. I'd saved my company.

I turned and looked hard at my twin sisters. They spent half of every day crouched beside the telephone, waiting to pounce on it at the first ring. "Her name is Sarah," I said. "So if she calls, please . . . be nice."

Weeks later I came home from running errands and there she was, in my living room, sitting with my mother and sisters. "Surprise," she said. She'd gotten my note and decided to take me up on my offer. She'd phoned from the airport and my sister Joanne had answered and shown what sisters are for. She promptly drove out to the airport and fetched Sarah.

I laughed. We hugged, awkwardly, my mother and sisters watching. "Let's go for a walk," I said.

I got her a jacket from my room and we walked in a light rain to a wooded park nearby. She saw Mount Hood in the distance and agreed that it looked astonishingly like Fuji, which made us both reminisce.

I asked where she was staying. "Silly boy," she said.

For two weeks she lived in my parents' guest room, just like one of the family, which I began to think she might one day be. I watched in disbelief as she charmed the uncharmable Knights. My protective sisters, my shy mother, my autocratic father, they were no match for her. Especially my father. When she shook his hand, she melted something hard at his core. Maybe it was growing up among the Candy Bar People and all their mogul friends—she had the kind of self-confidence you run across once or twice in a lifetime.

She was certainly the only person I'd ever known who could casually drop Babe Paley and Hermann Hesse into the same conversation. She admired them both. But especially Hesse. She was going to write a book about him one day. "It's like Hesse says," she purred over dinner one night, "happiness is a *how*, not a *what*."

The Knights chewed their pot roast, sipped their milk. "Very interesting," my father said.

I brought Sarah down to the worldwide headquarters of Blue Ribbon, in the basement, and showed her the operation. I gave her a pair of Limber Ups. She wore them when we drove out to the coast. We went hiking up Humbug Mountain, and crabbing along the scalloped coastline, and huckleberry picking in the woods. Standing under an eighty-foot spruce we shared a huckleberry kiss.

When it was time for her to fly back to Maryland, I was bereft. I wrote her every other day. My first-ever love letters. *Dear Sarah, I think about sitting beside that torii gate with you . . .*

She always wrote back right away. She always expressed her undying love.

That Christmas, 1964, she returned. This time I picked her up at the airport. On the way to my house she told me that there had been a terrible row before she got on the plane. Her parents forbade her to come. They didn't approve of me. "My father screamed," she said.

"What did he scream?" I asked.

She imitated his voice. "You can't meet a guy on Mount Fuji who's going to amount to anything."

I winced. I knew I had two strikes against me, but I didn't realize climbing Mount Fuji was one of them. What was so bad about climbing Mount Fuji?

"How did you get away?" I asked.

"My brother. He snuck me out of the house early this morning and drove me to the airport."

I wondered if she really loved me, or just saw me as a chance to rebel.

During the day, while I was busy working on Blue Ribbon stuff, Sarah would hang out with my mother. At night she and I would go downtown for dinner and drinks. On the weekend we skied Mount Hood. When it was time for her to return home, I was bereft again. *Dear Sarah, I miss you. I love you.*

89

She wrote back right away. She missed me, too. She loved me, too. Then, with the winter rains, there was a slight cooling in her letters. They were less effusive. Or so I thought. Maybe it's just my imagination, I told myself. But I had to know. I phoned her.

It wasn't my imagination. She said she'd given it a lot of thought and she wasn't sure we were right for each other. She wasn't sure I was sophisticated enough for her. "Sophisticated," that was the word she used. Before I could protest, before I could negotiate, she hung up.

I took out a piece of paper and typed her a long letter, begging her to reconsider.

She wrote back right away. No sale.

The new shipment of shoes arrived from Onitsuka. I could hardly bring myself to care. I spent weeks in a fog. I hid in the basement. I hid in the servants' quarters. I lay on my bed and stared at my blue ribbons.

Though I didn't tell them, my family knew. They didn't ask for details. They didn't need them, or want them.

Except my sister Jeanne. While I was out one day she went into the servants' quarters and into my desk and found Sarah's letters. Later, when I came home and went down to the basement, Jeanne came and found me. She sat on the floor beside me and said she'd read the letters, all of them, carefully, concluding with the final rejection. I looked away. "You're better off without her," Jeanne said.

My eyes filled with tears. I nodded thanks. Not knowing what to say, I asked Jeanne if she'd like to do some part-time work for Blue Ribbon. I was pretty far behind, and I could sure use some help. "Since you're so interested in mail," I said hoarsely, "maybe you'd enjoy doing some secretarial work. Dollar and a half an hour?"

She chuckled.

And thus my sister became the first-ever employee of Blue Ribbon.

1965

got a letter from that Jeff Johnson fellow at the start of the year. After our chance meeting at Occidental, I'd sent him a pair of Tigers, as a gift, and now he wrote to say that he'd tried them on and gone for a run. He liked them, he said. He liked them a whole lot. Others liked them, too. People kept stopping him and pointing at his feet and asking where they could buy some neat shoes like those.

Johnson had gotten married since I last saw him, he said, and there was already a baby on the way, so he was looking for ways to earn extra cash, apart from his gig as a social worker, and this Tiger shoe seemed to have more upside than Adidas. I wrote him back and offered him a post as a "commissioned salesman." Meaning I'd give him $1.75 for each pair of running shoes he sold, two bucks for each pair of spikes. I was just beginning to put together a crew of part-time sales reps, and that was the standard rate I was offering.

He wrote back right away, accepting the offer.

And then the letters didn't stop. On the contrary, they increased. In length and number. At first they were two pages. Then four. Then eight. At first they came every few days. Then they came faster, and faster, tumbling almost daily through the mail slot like a waterfall, each one with that same return address, P.O. Box 492, Seal Beach, CA 90740, until I wondered what in God's name I'd done in hiring this guy.

I liked his energy, of course. And it was hard to fault his enthusiasm. But I began to worry that he might have too much of each. With the twentieth letter, or the twenty-fifth, I began to worry that the man might be unhinged. I wondered why everything was so breathless. I wondered if he was ever going to run out of things he urgently needed to tell me or ask me. I wondered if he was ever going to run out of stamps.

Every time a thought crossed Johnson's mind, seemingly, he wrote it down and stuck it into an envelope. He wrote to tell me how many Tigers he'd sold that week. He wrote to tell me how many Tigers he'd sold that day. He wrote to tell me who'd worn Tigers at which high school meet and in what place they'd finished. He wrote to say that he wanted to expand his sales territory beyond California, to include Arizona, and possibly New Mexico. He wrote to suggest that we open a retail store in Los Angeles. He wrote to tell me that he was considering placing ads in running magazines and what did I think? He wrote to inform me that he'd placed those ads in running magazines and the response was good. He wrote to ask why I hadn't answered any of his previous letters. He wrote to plead for encouragement. He wrote to complain that I hadn't responded to his previous plea for encouragement.

I'd always considered myself a conscientious correspondent. (I'd sent countless letters and postcards home during my trip around the world. I'd written faithfully to Sarah.) And I always meant to answer Johnson's letters. But before I got around to it there was always another one, waiting. Something about the sheer volume of his correspondence stopped me. Something about his neediness made me not want to encourage him. Many nights I'd sit down at the black Royal typewriter in my basement workshop, curl a piece of paper into the roller, and type, *Dear Jeff*. Then I'd draw a blank. I wouldn't know where to begin, which of his fifty questions to start with, so I'd get up, attend to other things, and the next day there'd be yet another letter from Johnson. Or two. Soon I'd be three letters behind, suffering from crippling writer's block.

I asked Jeanne to deal with the "Johnson File." Fine, she said.

Within a month she thrust the file at me, exasperated. "You're not paying me enough," she said.

At some point I stopped reading Johnson's letters all the way to the bottom. But from skimming them I learned that he was selling Tigers part-time and on weekends, that he'd decided to keep his day job as a social worker for Los Angeles County. I still couldn't fathom it. Johnson just didn't strike me as a people person. In fact, he'd always seemed somewhat misanthropic. It was one of the things I'd liked about him.

In April 1965 he wrote to say he'd quit his day job. He'd always hated it, he said, but the last straw had been a distressed woman in the San Fernando Valley. He'd been scheduled to check on her, because she'd threatened to kill herself, but he'd phoned her first to ask "if she really was going to kill herself that day." If so, he didn't want to waste the time and gas money driving all the way out to the valley. The woman, and Johnson's superiors, took a dim view of his approach. They deemed it a sign that Johnson didn't care. Johnson deemed it the same way. He *didn't* care, and in that moment, Johnson wrote me, he understood himself, and his destiny. Social work wasn't it. He wasn't put here on this earth to fix people's problems. He preferred to focus on their feet.

In his heart of hearts Johnson believed that runners are God's chosen, that running, done right, in the correct spirit and with the proper form, is a mystical exercise, no less than meditation or prayer, and thus he felt called to help runners reach their nirvana. I'd been around runners much of my life, but this kind of dewy romanticism was something I'd never encountered. Not even the Yahweh of running, Bowerman, was as pious about the sport as Blue Ribbon's Part-Time Employee Number Two.

In fact, in 1965, running wasn't even a sport. It wasn't popular, it wasn't unpopular—it just was. To go out for a three-mile run was something weirdos did, presumably to burn off manic energy. Running for pleasure, running for exercise, running for endorphins, running to live better and longer—these things were unheard of.

People often went out of their way to mock runners. Drivers would slow down and honk their horns. "Get a horse!" they'd yell, throwing a soda or other trash at the runner's head. Johnson had been drenched by many a Pepsi. He wanted to change all this. He wanted to help all the oppressed runners of the world, to bring them into the light, enfold them in a community. So maybe he was a social worker after all. He just wanted to socialize exclusively with runners.

Above all, Johnson wanted to make a living doing it, which was next to impossible in 1965. In me, in Blue Ribbon, he thought he saw a way.

I did everything I could to discourage Johnson from thinking like this. At every turn I tried to dampen his enthusiasm for me and my company. Besides not writing back, I never phoned, never visited, never invited him to Oregon. I also never missed an opportunity to tell him the unvarnished truth. In one of my rare replies to his letters I put it flatly: *Though our growth has* *been good, I owe First National Bank of Oregon $11,000. . . . Cash flow is negative.*

He wrote back immediately, asking if he could work for me full-time. *I want to be able to make it on Tiger, and the opportunity would exist for me to do other things as well—running, school, not to mention being my own boss.*

I shook my head. I tell the man Blue Ribbon is sinking like the *Titanic*, and he responds by begging for a berth in first class.

Oh well, I thought, if we do go down, misery loves company.

So in the late summer of 1965 I wrote and accepted Johnson's offer to become the first *full-time* employee of Blue Ribbon. We negotiated his salary via the mail. He'd been making $460 a month as a social worker, but he said he could live on $400. I agreed. Reluctantly. It seemed exorbitant, but Johnson was so scattered, so flighty, and Blue Ribbon was so tenuous— one way or another I figured it was temporary.

As ever, the accountant in me saw the risk, the entrepreneur saw the possibility. So I split the difference and kept moving forward.

And then I stopped thinking about Johnson altogether. I had bigger problems at the moment. My banker was upset with me.

After posting eight thousand dollars in sales in my first

year, I was projecting sixteen thousand dollars in my second year, and according to my banker, this was a very troubling trend.

"A one hundred percent increase in sales is *troubling?*" I asked.

"Your rate of growth is too fast for your equity," he said.

"How can such a small company grow too fast? If a small company grows fast, it *builds up* its equity."

"It's all the same principle, regardless of size," he said. "Growth off your balance sheet is dangerous."

"Life is growth," I said. "Business is growth. You grow or you die."

"That's not how we see it."

"You might as well tell a runner in a race that he's running too fast."

"Apples and oranges."

Your head is full of apples and oranges, I wanted to say.

It was textbook to me. Growing sales, plus profitability, plus unlimited upside equals quality company. In those days, however, commercial banks were different from investment banks. Their myopic focus was cash balances. They wanted you to never, ever outgrow your cash balance.

Again and again I'd gently try to explain the shoe business to my banker. If I don't keep growing, I'd say, I won't be able to persuade Onitsuka that I'm the best man to distribute their shoes in the West. If I can't persuade Onitsuka that I'm the best, they'll find some other guy to take my place. And that doesn't even take into account the battle with the biggest monster out there, Adidas.

My banker was unmoved. Unlike Athena, he did not admire my eyes of persuasion. "Mr. Knight," he'd say again and again, "you need to slow down. You don't have enough equity for this kind of growth."

Equity. How I was beginning to loathe this word. My banker used it over and over, until it became a tune I couldn't get out of my head. Equity—I heard it while brushing my teeth in the morning. Equity—I heard it while punching my pillow at night. Equity—I reached the point where I refused to even say it aloud, because it wasn't a real word, it was bureaucratic jargon, a euphemism for cold hard *cash*, of which I had none. Purposely. Any dollar that wasn't nailed down I was plowing directly back into the business. Was that so rash?

To have cash balances sitting around doing nothing made no sense to me. Sure, it would have been the cautious, conservative, prudent thing. But the roadside was littered with cautious, conservative, prudent entrepreneurs. I wanted to keep my foot pressed hard on the gas pedal.

Somehow, in meeting after meeting, I held my tongue. Everything my banker said, I ultimately accepted. Then I'd do exactly as I pleased. I'd place another order with Onitsuka, double the size of the previous order, and show up at the bank all wide-eyed innocence, asking for a letter of credit to cover it. My banker would always be shocked. *You want HOW much?* And I'd always pretend to be shocked that he was shocked. *I thought you'd see the wisdom . . .* I'd wheedle, grovel, negotiate, and eventually he'd approve my loan.

After I'd sold out the shoes, and repaid the borrowing in full, I'd do it all over again. Place a mega order with Onitsuka, double the size of the previous order, then go to the bank in my best suit, an angelic look on my face.

My banker's name was Harry White. Fiftyish, avuncular, with a voice like a handful of gravel in a blender, he didn't seem to want to be a banker, and he particularly didn't want to be *my* banker. He inherited me by default. My first banker had been Ken Curry, but when my father refused to be my guarantor, Curry phoned him straightaway. "Between us, Bill, if the kid's company goes under—you'll still back him, right?"

"Hell no," my father said.

So Curry decided he wanted no part of this father-son internecine war and turned me over to White.

White was a vice president at First National, but this title was misleading. He didn't have much power. The bosses were always looking over his shoulder, second-guessing him, and the bossiest of bosses was a man named Bob Wallace. It was Wallace who made life difficult for White, and thereby for me. It was Wallace who fetishized equity and pooh-poohed growth.

Squarely built, with a thuggish face and Nixonian five o'clock shadow, Wallace was ten years my senior, but somehow thought himself the bank's boy wonder. He was also determined to become the bank's next president, and he viewed all bad credit risks as the main roadblock between him and that goal. He didn't like giving credit to anyone, for anything, but with my balance hovering always around zero, he saw me as a disaster waiting to happen. One slow season, one downturn in sales, I'd be out of business, the lobby of Wallace's bank would be filled with my unsold shoes, and the holy grail of bank president would slip from his grasp. Like Sarah atop Mount Fuji, Wallace saw me as a rebel, but he didn't think of this as a compliment. Nor, in the end, come to think of it, had she.

Of course, Wallace didn't always say all this directly to me. It was often conveyed by his middleman, White. White believed in me, and in Blue Ribbon, but he'd tell me all the time, with a sad head shake, that Wallace made the decisions, Wallace signed the checks, and Wallace was no fan of Phil Knight. I thought it was fitting, and telling, and hopeful, that White would use that word—"fan." He was tall, lean, a former athlete who loved to talk sports. No wonder we saw eye to eye. Wallace, on the other hand, looked as if he'd never set foot on a ball field. Unless maybe to repossess the equipment.

What sweet satisfaction it would have been to tell Wallace

where he could shove his equity, then storm out and take my business elsewhere. But in 1965 there was no elsewhere. First National Bank was the only game in town and Wallace knew it. Oregon was smaller back then, and it had just two banks, First National and U.S. Bank. The latter had already turned me down. If I got thrown out of the former, I'd be done. (Today you can live in one state and bank in another, no problem, but banking regulations were much tighter in those days.)

Also, there was no such thing as venture capital. An aspiring young entrepreneur had very few places to turn, and those places were all guarded by risk-averse gatekeepers with zero imagination. In other words, bankers. Wallace was the rule, not the exception.

To make everything more difficult, Onitsuka was always late shipping my shoes, which meant less time to sell, which meant less time to make enough money to cover my loan. When I complained, Onitsuka didn't answer. When they did answer, they failed to appreciate my quandary. Time and again I'd send them a frantic telex, inquiring about the whereabouts of the latest shipment, and in response I'd typically get a telex that was maddeningly obtuse. *Little more days.* It was like dialing 911 and hearing someone on the other end yawn.

Given all these problems, given Blue Ribbon's cloudy future, I decided that I'd better get a real job, something safe to fall back on when everything went bust. At the same moment

Johnson devoted himself exclusively to Blue Ribbon, I decided to branch out.

By now I'd passed all four parts of the CPA exam. So I mailed my test results and résumé to several local firms, interviewed with three or four, and got hired by Price Waterhouse. Like it or not, I was officially and irrevocably a card-carrying bean counter. My tax returns for that year wouldn't list my occupation as self-employed, or business owner, or entrepreneur. They would identify me as Philip H. Knight, Accountant.

Most days I didn't mind. For starters, I invested a healthy portion of my paycheck into Blue Ribbon's account at the bank, padding my precious equity, boosting the company's cash balance. Also, unlike Lybrand, the Portland branch of Price Waterhouse was a midsize firm. It had some thirty accountants on staff, compared to Lybrand's four, which made it a better fit for me.

The work suited me better, too. Price Waterhouse boasted a great variety of clients, a mix of interesting start-ups and established companies, all selling everything imaginable— lumber, water, power, food. While auditing these companies, digging into their guts, taking them apart and putting them back together, I was also learning how they survived, or didn't. How they sold things, or didn't. How they got into trouble, how they got out. I took careful notes about what made companies tick, what made them fail.

Again and again I learned that lack of equity was a leading cause of failure.

The accountants worked in teams, generally, and the A-Team was headed by Delbert J. Hayes, the best accountant in the office, and by far its most flamboyant character. Six foot two, three hundred pounds, most of it stuffed sausagelike into an exceedingly inexpensive polyester suit, Hayes possessed great talent, great wit, great passion—and great appetites. Nothing gave him more pleasure than laying waste to a hoagie and a drink, unless it was doing both while studying a spreadsheet.

I'd met other accountants who knew numbers, who had a way with numbers, but Hayes was to the numbers born. In a column of otherwise unspectacular fours and nines and twos, he could discern the raw elements of Beauty. He looked at numbers the way the poet looks at clouds, the way the geologist looks at rocks. He could draw from them rhapsodic song, demotic truths.

And uncanny predictions. Hayes could use numbers to tell the future.

Day after day I watched Hayes do something I'd never thought possible: He made accounting an art. Which meant he, and I, and all of us, were artists. It was a wonderful thought, an ennobling thought, one that would have never occurred to me.

Intellectually I always knew that numbers were beautiful. On some level I understood that numbers represented a secret code, that behind every row of numbers lay ethereal Platonic forms. My accounting classes had taught me that, sort of. As had sports. Running track gives you a fierce respect for numbers, because you *are* what your numbers say you are, nothing more, nothing less. If I posted a bad time in a race, there might have been reasons—injury, fatigue, broken heart—but no one cared. My numbers, in the end, were all that anyone would remember. I'd lived this reality, but Hayes the artist made me feel it.

Alas, I came to fear that Hayes was the tragic kind of artist, the self-sabotaging, Van Gogh kind. He undercut himself at the firm, every day, by dressing badly, slouching badly, behaving badly. He also had an array of phobias—heights, snakes, bugs, confined spaces—which could be off-putting to his bosses and colleagues.

But he was most phobic about diets. Price Waterhouse would have made Hayes a partner, without hesitation, but the firm couldn't overlook his weight. It wasn't going to tolerate a three-hundred-pound partner. More than likely it was this unhappy fact that made Hayes eat so much in the first place. Whatever the reason, he ate a lot.

Come quitting time, he would recount his endless stories

to junior accountants. He talked nonstop, and some of the other accountants called him Uncle Remus. But I never did. I never rolled my eyes at Hayes's stem-winders. Each story contained some gem of wisdom about business—what made companies work, what the ledgers of a company really *meant*.

It didn't help that, when I wasn't a foot soldier in Hayes's Army, I was still serving in the Reserves. (A seven-year commitment.) Tuesday nights, from seven to ten, I had to throw a switch in my brain and become First Lieutenant Knight. My unit was composed of longshoremen, and we were often stationed in the warehouse district, a few football fields away from where I picked up my shipments from Onitsuka. Most nights my men and I would load and unload ships, maintain jeeps and trucks. Many nights we'd do PT—physical training. Push-ups, pull-ups, sit-ups, running. I remember one night I led my company on a four-mile run. I set a killing pace, and steadily increased it, grinding myself and the men to dust. After, I overheard one panting soldier tell another: "I was listening real close as Lieutenant Knight counted cadence. I never once heard that man take a deep breath!"

It was perhaps my only triumph of 1965.

Some Tuesday nights in the Reserves were set aside for classroom time. Instructors would talk to us about military strategy, which I found riveting. The instructors would often begin class by dissecting some long-ago, famous battle. But invariably they would drift off topic, onto Vietnam. The conflict was getting hotter. The United States was being drawn toward it, inexorably, as if by a giant magnet.

I had grown to hate that war. Not simply because I felt it was wrong. I also felt it was stupid, wasteful. I hated stupidity. I hated waste. Above all, *that* war, more than other wars, seemed to be run along the same principles as my bank. Fight not to win, but to avoid losing. A surefire losing strategy.

Now and then Hayes would hit the road, visit clients across Oregon, and I frequently found myself part of his traveling medicine show. Of all his junior accountants, I might have been his favorite, but especially when he traveled.

On one of those road trips, I told Hayes about Blue Ribbon. He saw promise in it. He also saw doom. The numbers, he said, didn't lie. "Starting a new company," he said, "in this economy? And a shoe company? With zero cash balance?" He slouched and shook his big fuzzy head.

On the other hand, he said, I had one thing in my favor. Bowerman. A legend for a partner—that was one asset for which it was impossible to assign a number.

Plus, my asset was rising in value. Bowerman had gone to Japan for the 1964 Olympics, to support the members of the U.S. track-and-field team he'd coached. (Two of his runners,

Bill Dellinger and Harry Jerome, medaled.) And after the Games, Bowerman had switched hats and become an ambassador for Blue Ribbon. He and Mrs. Bowerman—whose Christmas Club account had provided the initial five hundred dollars Bowerman gave me to form our partnership—visited Onitsuka and charmed everyone in the building.

They were given a royal welcome, a VIP tour of the factory, and Morimoto even introduced them to Mr. Onitsuka. The two old lions, of course, bonded. Both, after all, were built from the same last, shaped by the same war. Both still approached everyday life as a battle. Mr. Onitsuka, however, had the particular tenacity of the defeated, which impressed Bowerman. Mr. Onitsuka told Bowerman about founding his shoe company in the ruins of Japan, when all the big cities were still smoldering from American bombs. He'd built his first lasts, for a line of basketball shoes, by pouring hot wax from Buddhist candles over his own feet. Though the basketball shoes didn't sell, Mr. Onitsuka didn't give up. He simply switched to running shoes, and the rest was shoe history. Every Japanese runner in the 1964 Games, Bowerman told me, was wearing Tigers.

Mr. Onitsuka also told Bowerman that the inspiration for the unique soles on Tigers had come to him while eating sushi. Looking down at his wooden platter, at the underside of an octopus's leg, he thought a similar suction cup might work on the sole of a runner's flat. Bowerman filed that away. Inspiration, he learned, can come from quotidian things. Things you might eat. Or find lying around the house.

Now back in Oregon, Bowerman was happily corresponding with his new friend, Mr. Onitsuka, and with the entire production team at the Onitsuka factory. He was sending them bunches of ideas and modifications of their products. Though all people are the same under the skin, Bowerman had come to believe that all feet are not created equal. Americans have different bodies than Japanese do—longer, heavier—and Americans therefore need different shoes. After dissecting a dozen pairs of Tigers, Bowerman saw how they could be tailored to cater to American customers. To that end, he had a slew of notes, sketches, designs, all of which he was firing off to Japan.

Sadly, he was discovering, as I had, that no matter how well you got along in person with the team at Onitsuka, things were different once you were back on your side of the Pacific. Most of Bowerman's letters went unanswered. When there was an answer, it was cryptic, or curtly dismissive. It pained me at times to think the Japanese were treating Bowerman the way I was treating Johnson.

But Bowerman wasn't me. He didn't take rejection to heart. Like Johnson, when his letters went unanswered, Bowerman simply wrote more. With more underlined words, more exclamation marks.

Nor did he flag in his experiments. He continued to tear apart Tigers, continued to use the young men on his track teams as lab mice. During the autumn track season of 1965, every race had two results for Bowerman. There was the performance of his runners, and there was the performance of their shoes. Bowerman would note how the arches held up, how the soles gripped the cinders, how the toes pinched and the instep flexed. Then he'd airmail his notes and findings to Japan.

Eventually he broke through. Onitsuka made prototypes that conformed to Bowerman's vision of a more American shoe. Soft inner sole, more arch support, heel wedge to reduce stress on the Achilles tendon—they sent the prototype to Bowerman and he went wild for it. He asked for more. He then handed these experimental shoes out to all his runners, who used them to crush the competition.

A little success always went to Bowerman's head, in the best way. Around this time he was also testing sports elixirs, magic potions and powders to give his runners more energy and stamina. When I was on his team he'd talked about the importance of replacing an athlete's salt and electrolytes. He'd forced me and others to choke down a potion he'd invented, a vile goo of mushed bananas, lemonade, tea, honey, and several unnamed ingredients. Now, while tinkering with shoes, he was also monkeying with his sports drink recipe, making it taste worse and work better. It wasn't until years later that

I realized Bowerman was trying to invent Gatorade.

In his "free time," he liked to noodle with the surface at Hayward Field. Hayward was hallowed ground, steeped in tradition, but Bowerman didn't believe in letting tradition slow you down. Whenever rain fell, which it did all the time in Eugene, Hayward's cinder lanes turned to Venetian canals. Bowerman thought something rubbery would be easier to dry, sweep, and clean. He also thought something rubbery might be more forgiving on his runners' feet. So he bought a cement mixer, filled it with old shredded tires and assorted chemicals, and spent hours searching for just the right consistency and texture. More than once he made himself violently sick from inhaling the fumes of this witches' brew. Blinding headaches, a pronounced limp, loss of vision—these were a few of the lasting costs of his perfectionism.

Again, it was years before I realized what Bowerman was actually up to. He was trying to invent polyurethane.

I once asked him how he fit everything into a twenty-four-hour day. Coaching, traveling, experimenting, raising a family. He grunted as if to say, *It's nothing.* Then he told me, sotto voce, that on top of everything else, he was also writing a book.

"A book?" I said.

"About jogging," he said gruffly.

Bowerman was forever griping that people make the

mistake of thinking only elite Olympians are athletes. But everyone's an athlete, he said. If you have a body, you're an athlete. Now he was determined to get this point across to a larger audience. The reading public. "Sounds interesting," I said, but I thought my old coach had popped a screw. Who in heck would want to read a book about jogging?

1966

As I neared the end of my contract with Onitsuka, I checked the mail every day, hoping for a letter that would say they wanted to renew. Or that they didn't. There would be relief in knowing either way. Of course I was also hoping for a letter from Sarah, saying she'd changed her mind. And as always I was braced for a letter from my bank, telling me my business was no longer welcome.

But every day the only letters were from Johnson. Like Bowerman, the man didn't sleep. Ever. I could think of no other explanation for his ceaseless stream of correspondence. Much of which was pointless. Along with gobs of information I didn't need, the typical Johnson letter would include several long parenthetical asides, and some kind of rambling joke.

There might also be a hand-drawn illustration. There might also be a musical lyric.

Sometimes there was a poem.

Batted out on a manual typewriter that violently Brailled

the onionskin pages, many Johnson letters contained some kind of story. Maybe "parable" is a better word. How Johnson had sold this person a pair of Tigers, but down the road said person might be good for X more pairs, and therefore Johnson had a plan.... How Johnson had chased and badgered the head coach at such-and-such high school and tried to sell him *six pairs*, but in the end sold him a *baker's dozen* ... which just went to show ...

Often Johnson would describe in excruciating detail the latest ad he'd placed or was contemplating placing in the back pages of *Long Distance Log* or *Track & Field News*. Or he'd describe the photograph of a Tiger shoe he'd included with the ad. He'd constructed a makeshift photo studio in his house, and he'd pose the shoes seductively on the sofa, against a black sweater. I just didn't see the point of placing ads in magazines read exclusively by running nerds. I didn't see the point of advertising, period. But Johnson seemed to be having fun, and he swore the ads worked, so, fine, far be it from me to stop him.

The typical Johnson letter would invariably close with a lament, either sarcastic or pointedly earnest, about my failure to respond to his previous letter. And the one before that, etc. Then there would be a PS, and usually another PS, and sometimes a pagoda of PS's. Then one last plea for encouraging words, which I never sent. I didn't have time for encouraging words. Besides, it wasn't my style.

I look back now and wonder if I was truly being myself,

or if I was emulating Bowerman or my father, or both. Was I adopting their man-of-few-words demeanor? Was I maybe modeling all the men I admired? At the time I was reading everything I could get my hands on about generals, samurai, shoguns, along with biographies of my three main heroes—Churchill, Kennedy, and Tolstoy. I had no love of violence, but I was fascinated by leadership, or lack thereof, under extreme conditions. War is the most extreme of conditions. But business has its warlike parallels. Someone somewhere once said that business is war without bullets, and I tended to agree.

I wasn't that unique. Throughout history men have looked to the warrior for a model of Hemingway's cardinal virtue, pressurized grace. (Hemingway himself wrote most of *A Moveable Feast* while gazing at a statue of Marshal Ney, Napoléon's favorite commander.) One lesson I took from all my homeschooling about heroes was that they didn't say much. None was a blabbermouth. None micromanaged. *Don't tell people how to do things, tell them what to do and let them surprise you with their results.* So I didn't answer Johnson, and I didn't pester him. Having told him what to do, I hoped that he would surprise me.

Maybe with silence.

To Johnson's credit, though he craved more communication, he never let the lack of it discourage him. On the contrary, it motivated him. He was beyond detail oriented, he recognized that I was not, and though he enjoyed complaining (to me, to my sister, to mutual friends), he saw that my managerial style gave him freedom. Left to do as he pleased, he responded with boundless creativity and energy. He worked seven days a week, selling and promoting Blue Ribbon, and when he wasn't selling, he was beaverishly building up his customer data files.

Each new customer got his or her own index card, and each index card contained that customer's personal information, shoe size, and shoe preferences. This database enabled Johnson to keep in touch with all his customers, at all times, and to keep them all feeling special. He sent them Christmas cards. He sent them birthday cards. He sent them notes of congratulation after they completed a big race or marathon. Whenever I got a letter from Johnson I knew it was one of dozens he'd carried down to the mailbox that day. He had hundreds and hundreds of customer-correspondents, all along the spectrum of humanity, from high school track stars to octogenarian weekend joggers. Many, upon pulling yet another Johnson letter from their mailboxes, must have thought the same thing I did: *Where does this guy find the time?*

Unlike me, however, most customers came to depend on Johnson's letters. Most wrote him back. They'd tell him about their lives, their troubles, their injuries, and Johnson would lavishly console, sympathize, and advise. Especially about injuries. Few in the 1960s knew the first thing about running injuries, or sports injuries in general, so Johnson's letters were often filled with information that was impossible to find anywhere else. I worried briefly about liability issues. I also worried that I'd one day get a letter saying Johnson had rented a bus and was driving them all to the doctor.

Some customers freely volunteered their opinion about Tigers, so Johnson began aggregating this customer feedback, using it to create new design sketches. One man, for instance, complained that Tiger flats didn't have enough cushion. He wanted to run the Boston Marathon but didn't think Tigers would last the twenty-six miles. So Johnson hired a local cobbler to graft rubber soles from a pair of shower shoes into a pair of Tiger flats. Voilà. Johnson's Frankenstein flat had space-age, full-length, midsole cushioning. (Today it's standard in all training shoes for runners.) The jerry-rigged Johnson sole was so dynamic, so soft, so new, Johnson's customer posted a personal best in Boston. Johnson forwarded me the results and urged me to pass them along to Tiger. Bowerman had just asked me to do the same with his batch of notes a few weeks earlier. Good grief, I thought, one mad genius at a time.

Every now and then I'd make a mental note to warn Johnson about his growing list of pen pals. Blue Ribbon was supposed to confine itself to the thirteen western states, and Full-Time

Employee Number One was not doing so. Johnson had customers in thirty-seven states, including the entire Eastern Seaboard, which was the heart of East Coast Cowboy country. The East Coast Cowboy wasn't doing anything with his territory, so Johnson's incursions *seemed* harmless. But we didn't want to rub the man's nose in it.

Still, I never got around to telling Johnson my concerns. Per usual, I didn't tell him anything.

At the start of summer I decided my parents' basement was no longer big enough to serve as the headquarters of Blue Ribbon. And the servants' quarters weren't big enough for me. I rented a one-bedroom apartment downtown, in a spiffy new high-rise. The rent was two hundred dollars, which seemed pretty steep, but oh well. I also rented a few essentials—table, chairs, king-size bed, olive couch—and tried to arrange them stylishly. It didn't look like much, but I didn't care, because my real furniture was shoes. My first-ever bachelor pad was filled from floor to ceiling with shoes.

I toyed with the idea of not giving Johnson my new address. But I did.

Sure enough, my new mailbox began to fill with letters. Return address: P.O. Box 492, Seal Beach, CA 90740.

None of which I answered.

• • •

Then Johnson wrote me two letters I couldn't ignore. First, he said that he, too, was moving. He and his new wife were splitting up. He was planning to stay in Seal Beach, but taking a small bachelor apartment.

Days later he wrote to say he'd been in a car wreck.

It happened in the early morning, somewhere north of San Bernardino. He was on his way to a road race, of course, where he'd intended to both run and sell Tigers. He'd fallen asleep at the wheel, he wrote, and woke to find himself and his 1956 Volkswagen Bug upside down and airborne. He struck the divider, then rolled, then flew out of the car, just before it somersaulted down the embankment. When Johnson's body finally stopped tumbling, he was on his back, looking at the sky, his collarbone, foot, and skull all shattered.

The skull, he said, was actually leaking.

Worse, being newly divorced, he had no one to care for him during his convalescence.

The poor guy was one dead dog from becoming a country-western song.

Despite all these recent calamities, Johnson was of good cheer. He assured me in a series of chirpy follow-up letters that he was managing to meet all his obligations. He was dragging himself around his new apartment, filling orders, shipping shoes, corresponding promptly with all customers. A friend was bringing him his mail, he said, so not to worry, P.O. Box

492 was still fully operational. Then he added that because he was now facing alimony, child support, and untold medical bills, he needed to inquire about the long-term prospects of Blue Ribbon. How did I see the future?

I didn't lie . . . exactly. Maybe out of pity, maybe haunted by the image of Johnson, single, lonely, his body wrapped in plaster of Paris, gamely trying to keep himself and my company alive, I sounded an upbeat tone. Blue Ribbon, I said, would probably morph over the years into a generalized sporting goods company. We'd probably have offices on the West Coast. And one day, maybe, in Japan. *Farfetched,* I wrote. *But it seems worth shooting for.*

This last line was wholly truthful. It was worth shooting for. If Blue Ribbon went bust, I'd have no money, and I'd be crushed. But I'd also have some valuable wisdom, which I could apply to the next business. Wisdom seemed an intangible asset, but an asset all the same, one that justified the risk. Starting my own business was the only thing that made life's other risks—marriage, Vegas, alligator wrestling—seem like sure things. But my hope was that when I failed, if I failed, I'd fail quickly, so I'd have enough time, enough years, to implement all the hard-won lessons. I wasn't much for setting goals, but this goal kept flashing through my mind every day, until it became my internal chant: *Fail fast.*

In closing I told Johnson that if he could sell 3,250 pairs of

Tigers by the end of June 1966—completely impossible, by my calculations—I would authorize him to open that retail outlet he'd been harassing me about. I even put a PS at the bottom, which I knew he'd devour like a candy treat. I reminded him that he was selling so many shoes, so fast, he might want to speak to an accountant. There are income tax issues to consider, I said.

He fired back a sarcastic thanks for the tax advice. He wouldn't be filing taxes, he said, "because gross income was $1,209 while expenses total $1,245." His leg broken, his heart broken, he told me that he was also flat broke. He signed off: *Please send encouraging words.*

I didn't.

Somehow, Johnson hit the magic number. By the end of June he'd sold 3,250 pairs of Tigers. And he'd healed. Thus, he was holding me to my end of the bargain. Before Labor Day he leased a small retail space at 3107 Pico Boulevard, in Santa Monica, and opened our first-ever retail store.

He then set about turning the store into a mecca, a holy of holies for runners. He bought the most comfortable chairs he could find, and afford (yard sales), and he created a beautiful space for runners to hang out and talk. He built shelves and filled them with books that every runner should read, many of them first editions from his own library. He covered the walls with photos of Tiger-shod runners, and laid in a supply of silk-screened T-shirts with TIGER across the front, which he handed out to his best customers. He also stuck Tigers to a black lacquered wall and illuminated them with a strip of can lights—very hip. In all the world there had never been such a sanctuary for runners, a place that didn't just sell them shoes but celebrated them and their shoes. Johnson, the aspiring cult leader of runners, finally had his church. Services were Monday through Saturday, nine to six.

When he first wrote me about the store, I thought of the temples and shrines I'd seen in Asia, and I was anxious to see how Johnson's compared. But there just wasn't time. Between my hours at Price Waterhouse, my socializing with Hayes, my nights and weekends handling the minutiae connected with Blue Ribbon, and my fourteen hours each month soldiering in the Reserves, I was on fumes.

Then Johnson wrote me a fateful letter, and I had no choice. I jumped on a plane.

Johnson's customer pen pals now numbered in the hundreds, and one of them, a high school kid on Long Island, had written to Johnson and inadvertently revealed some troubling news. The kid said his track coach had recently been talking about acquiring Tigers from a new source . . . some wrestling coach in Valley Stream or Massapequa or Manhasset.

The East Coast Cowboy was back. He'd even placed a national ad in an issue of Track and Field. While Johnson was busy poaching on the East Coast Cowboy's turf, the East Coast Cowboy was poaching our poaching. Johnson had done all this marvelous groundwork, had built up this enormous customer base, had spread the word about Tigers through his doggedness and crude marketing, and now the East Coast Cowboy was going to swoop in and capitalize?

I'm not sure why I hopped on the next plane to Los Angeles. I could have phoned. Maybe, like Johnson's customers, I needed a sense of community, even if it was a community of just two.

The first thing we did was go for a long, punishing run on the beach. Then we bought a pizza and brought it back to his apartment, which was your standard Guy Pad, only more so. Tiny, dark, sparse—it reminded me of some of the no-frills hostels where I'd stayed on my trip around the world.

Of course there were a few distinctly Johnsonian touches. Like shoes everywhere. I thought my apartment was filled with shoes, but Johnson basically lived inside a running shoe. Shoved into every nook and cranny, spread across every surface, were running shoes, and more running shoes, most in some state of deconstruction.

The few nooks and crannies that didn't hold shoes were

filled with books, and more books, piled on homemade bookshelves, rough planks laid on cinder blocks. And Johnson didn't read trash. His collection was mostly thick volumes of philosophy, religion, sociology, anthropology, and the classics of Western literature. I thought I loved to read; Johnson was next level.

What struck me most was the eerie violet light that suffused the whole place. Its source was a 75-gallon saltwater fish tank. After clearing a place for me on the sofa, Johnson patted the tank and explained. Most newly divorced guys like to get out and meet people, but Johnson spent his nights under the Seal Beach pier, looking for rare fish. He captured them with something called a "slurp gun," which he waved under my nose. It looked like a prototype for the first-ever vacuum cleaner. I asked how it worked. Just stick this nozzle into shallow water, he said, and suck up the fish into a plastic tube, then into a small chamber. Then shoot it into your bucket and schlep it home.

He'd managed to accumulate a wide variety of exotic creatures—sea horses, opal-eye perch—which he showed me with pride. He pointed out the jewel of his collection, a baby octopus he'd named Stretch. "Speaking of which," Johnson said, "feeding time."

He reached into a paper sack and pulled out a live crab. "Come on, Stretch," he said, dangling the crab over the tank.

The octopus didn't stir. Johnson lowered the crab, legs wriggling, onto the tank's sand-strewn floor. Still no reaction from Stretch.

"He dead?" I asked.

"Watch," Johnson said.

The crab danced left and right, panicking, seeking cover. There was none, however. And Stretch knew it. After a few minutes something emerged tentatively from Stretch's undercarriage. An antenna or tentacle. It unfurled toward the crab and lightly tapped its carapace. Yoo-hoo? "Stretch just injected poison in the crab," Johnson said, grinning like a proud dad. We watched the crab slowly stop dancing, stop moving altogether. We watched Stretch gently wrap his antenna-tentacle around the crab and drag it back to his lair, a hole he'd dug into the sand beneath a big rock.

It was a morbid puppet show, a dark Kabuki play, starring a witless victim and a micro-kraken—was it a sign, a metaphor for our dilemma? One living thing being eaten by another? This was nature, wet in tooth and claw, and I couldn't help wondering if it was also to be the story of Blue Ribbon and the East Coast Cowboy.

We spent the rest of the evening sitting at Johnson's kitchen table and going over the letter from his Long Island informant. He read it aloud, and then I read it silently, and then we debated what to do.

"Get thee to Japan," Johnson said.

"What?"

"You gotta go," he said. "Tell them about the work we've done. Demand your rights. Kill this East Coast Cowboy once and for all. Once he starts selling running shoes, once he really gets going, there will be no stopping him. Either we draw a line in the sand, right now, or it's over."

I'd just come back from Japan, I said, and I didn't have the money to go again. I'd poured all my savings into Blue Ribbon, and I couldn't possibly ask Wallace for another loan. The thought nauseated me. Also, I didn't have time. Price Waterhouse allowed two weeks' vacation a year—unless you needed that two weeks for the Reserves, which I did. Then they gave you one extra week. Which I'd already used.

Above all, I told Johnson, "It's no use. The East Coast Cowboy's relationship with Onitsuka predates mine."

Undaunted, Johnson pulled out his typewriter, the one he'd been using to torture me, and began drafting notes, ideas, lists, which we could then turn into a manifesto for me to deliver to the executives at Onitsuka. While Stretch finished off the crab, we munched our pizza and plotted late into the night.

Back in Oregon the next afternoon, I went straight in to see the office manager at Price Waterhouse. "I've got to have two weeks off," I said, "right now."

He looked up from the papers on his desk and glared at me, and for one hellishly long moment I thought I was going to be fired. Instead, he cleared his throat and mumbled something . . . odd. I couldn't make out every word but he seemed to think . . . from my intensity, my vagueness . . . I was in some kind of serious trouble.

I took a step back and started to protest, then shut my mouth. Let the man think what he wants. So long as he gives me the time.

Running a hand through his thinning hair, he finally sighed and said: "Go. Good luck. Hope it all works out."

I put the airfare on my credit card. Twelve months to pay. And unlike my last visit to Japan, this time I wired ahead. I told the executives at Onitsuka that I was coming and that I wanted a meeting.

They wired back: Come ahead.

But their wire went on to say that I wouldn't be meeting with Morimoto. He was either fired or dead. There was a new export manager, the wire said.

His name was Kitami.

Kishikan. Japanese for déjà vu. Again I found myself boarding a flight for Japan. Again I found myself underlining and memorizing my copy of *How to Do Business with the Japanese.*

Again I found myself taking the train to Kobe, checking into the Newport, pacing in my room.

At zero hour I took a cab over to Onitsuka. I expected that we'd go into the old conference room, but no, they'd done some remodeling since my last visit. New conference room, they said. Sleeker, bigger, it had leather chairs instead of the old cloth ones, and a much longer table. More impressive, but less familiar. I felt disoriented, intimidated. It was like prepping for a meet at Oregon State and learning at the last minute that it had been moved to the Los Angeles Memorial Coliseum.

A man walked into the conference room and extended his hand. Kitami. His black shoes were brightly polished, his hair equally polished. Jet black, swept straight back, not a strand out of place. He was a great contrast to Morimoto, who always looked as if he'd dressed blindfolded. I was put off by Kitami's veneer, but suddenly he gave me a warm, ready smile, and encouraged me to sit, relax, tell him why I'd come, and now I got the distinct sense that, despite his slick appearance, he wasn't altogether sure of himself. He was in a brand-new job, after all. He didn't yet have much—equity. The word sprang to mind.

It occurred to me also that I had high value for Kitami. I wasn't a big client, but I wasn't small, either. Location is everything. I was selling shoes in *America*, a market vital to the future of Onitsuka. Maybe, just maybe, Kitami didn't want to lose me just yet. Maybe he wanted to hold on to me until they'd transitioned to the East Coast Cowboy. I was an asset, I was a credit, for the moment, which meant I might be holding better cards than I thought.

Kitami spoke more English than his predecessors, but with a thicker accent. My ear needed a few minutes to adjust as we chatted about my flight, the weather, sales. All the while other executives were filing in, joining us at the conference table. At last Kitami leaned back. "*Hai . . .*" He waited.

"Mr. Onitsuka?" I asked.

"Mr. Onitsuka will not be able to join us today," he said.

Damn. I was hoping to draw upon Mr. Onitsuka's fondness for me, not to mention his bond with Bowerman. But no. Alone, without allies, trapped in the unfamiliar conference room, I plunged ahead.

I told Kitami and the other executives that Blue Ribbon had done a remarkable job thus far. We'd sold out every order, while developing a robust customer base, and we expected this solid growth to continue. We had forty-four thousand dollars in sales for 1966, and projected to have eighty-four thousand dollars in 1967. I described our new store in Santa Monica, and laid out plans for other stores—for a big future. Then I leaned in. "We would very much like to be the exclusive U.S. distributor for Tiger's track-and-field line," I said. "And I think it is very much in Tiger's interest that we become that."

I didn't even mention the East Coast Cowboy.

I looked around the table. Grim faces. None grimmer than Kitami's. He said in a few terse words that this would not be possible. Onitsuka wanted for its U.S. distributor someone bigger, more established, a firm that could handle the work-load. A firm with offices on the East Coast.

"But, but," I spluttered, "Blue Ribbon *does* have offices on the East Coast."

Kitami rocked back in his chair. "Oh?"

"Yes," I said, "we're on the East Coast, the West Coast, and soon we may be in the Midwest. We can handle national distri-bution, no question." I looked around the table. The grim faces were becoming less grim.

"Well," Kitami said, "this change things."

He assured me that they would give my proposal careful consideration. So. *Hai.* Meeting adjourned.

I walked back to my hotel and spent a second night pacing. First thing the next morning I received a call summoning me back to Onitsuka, where Kitami awarded me exclusive distri-bution rights for the United States.

He gave me a three-year contract.

I tried to be nonchalant as I signed the papers and placed an order for five thousand more shoes, which would cost twenty thousand dollars I didn't have. Kitami said he'd ship them to my East Coast office, which I also didn't have.

I promised to wire him the exact address.

*   *   *

On the flight home I looked out the window at the clouds above the Pacific Ocean and thought back to sitting atop Mount Fuji. I wondered how Sarah would feel about me now, after this coup. I wondered how the East Coast Cowboy would feel when he got word from Onitsuka that he was toast.

I stowed away my copy of *How to Do Business with the Japanese*. My carry-on was stuffed with souvenirs. Kimonos for my mother and sisters and Mom Hatfield, a tiny samurai sword to hang above my desk. And my crowning glory: a small Japanese TV. Spoils of war, I thought, smiling. But somewhere over the Pacific the full weight of my "victory" came over me. I imagined the look on Wallace's face when I asked him to cover this gigantic new order. If he said no, *when* he said no, what then?

On the other hand, if he said yes, how was I going to open an office on the East Coast? And how was I going to do it before those shoes arrived? And who was I going to get to run it?

I stared at the curved, glowing horizon. There was only one person on the planet rootless enough, energetic enough, gung-ho enough, crazy enough to pick up and move to the East Coast, on a moment's notice, and get there before the shoes did.

I wondered how Stretch was going to like the Atlantic Ocean.

1967

didn't handle it well. Not well at all.

Knowing what his reaction would be, and dreading it, I put off telling Johnson the whole story. I shot him a quick note, saying the meeting with Onitsuka had gone fine, telling him I'd secured national distribution rights. But I left it at that. I think I must have held out hope, in the back of my mind, that I might be able to hire someone else to go east. Or that Wallace would blow the whole plan up.

And, in fact, I did hire someone else. A former distance runner, of course. But he changed his mind, backed out, just days after agreeing to go. So, frustrated, distracted, mired in a cycle of anxiety and procrastination, I turned to the much simpler problem of finding someone to replace Johnson at the store in Santa Monica. I asked John Bork, a high school track coach in Los Angeles, a friend of a friend. He jumped at the chance. He couldn't have been more eager. How could I have known he'd be quite so eager? The next morning he appeared at Johnson's store and announced that he was the new boss. "The new—what?" Johnson said.

"I've been hired to take over for you when you go back east," Bork said.

"When I go—where?" Johnson said, reaching for the phone.

I didn't handle that conversation well, either. I told Johnson that, ha-ha, hey, man, I was *just* about to call you. I said I was sorry he'd heard the news that way, how awkward, and I explained that I'd been forced to lie to Onitsuka and claim we already had an office on the East Coast. Thus, we were in one heck of a jam. The shoes would soon be on the water, an enormous shipment steaming for New York, and no one but Johnson could handle the task of claiming those shoes and setting up an office. The fate of Blue Ribbon rested on his shoulders.

Johnson was flabbergasted. Then furious. Then freaked. All in the space of one minute. So I got on a plane and flew down to visit him at his store.

He didn't want to live on the East Coast, he told me. He loved California. He'd lived in California all his life. He could go running year-round in California, and running, as I knew, was all to Johnson. How was he supposed to go running during those bitter cold winters back east? On and on it went.

All at once his manner changed. We were standing in the middle of his store, his sneaker sanctuary, and in a barely

133

audible mumble he acknowledged that this was a make-or-break moment for Blue Ribbon, in which he was heavily invested, financially, emotionally, spiritually. He acknowledged that there was no one else who could set up an East Coast office.

I kept my mouth shut and waited.

And waited.

"Okay," he said, at last, "I'll go."

"Great. That's great. Terrific. Thank you."

"But where?"

"Where what?"

"Do you want me to go?"

"Ah. Yes. Well. Anywhere on the East Coast with a port. Just don't go to Portland, Maine."

"Why?"

"A company based in two different Portlands? That'll confuse the heck out of the Japanese."

We hashed it out some more and finally decided New York and Boston were the most logical places. Especially Boston. "It's where most of our orders are coming from," one of us said.

"Okay," he said. "Boston, here I come."

Then I handed him a bunch of travel brochures for Boston, playing up the fall foliage angle. A little heavy-handed, but I was desperate.

He asked how I happened to have these brochures on me, and I told him I knew he'd make the right decision.

He laughed.

The forgiveness Johnson showed me, the overall good nature he demonstrated, filled me with gratitude, and a new fondness for the man. And perhaps a deeper loyalty. I regretted my treatment of him. All those unanswered letters. There are team players, I thought, and then there are team players, and then there's Johnson.

And then he threatened to quit.

Via letter, of course. *I think I have been responsible for what success we have had so far,* he wrote. *And any success that will be coming in for the next two years at least.*

Therefore, he gave me a two-part ultimatum:

1. Make him a full partner in Blue Ribbon.

2. Raise his salary to six hundred dollars a month, plus a third of all profits beyond the first six thousand pairs of shoes sold.

Or else, he said, good-bye.

I phoned Bowerman and told him that Full-Time Employee Number One was staging a mutiny. Bowerman listened quietly, considered all the angles, weighed the pros and cons, then rendered his verdict, which was basically: Who needs him.

I realized I needed Johnson. Maybe there was some middle way of mollifying Johnson, of giving him a stake in the company. But as we talked about it in greater detail, the math just didn't pencil out. Neither Bowerman nor I wanted to surrender any portion of our stake, so Johnson's ultimatum, even if I'd wanted to accept it, was a nonstarter.

I flew to Palo Alto, where Johnson was visiting his parents, and asked for a sit-down. Johnson said he wanted his father, Owen, to join us. The meeting took place at Owen's office, and I was immediately stunned by the similarities between father and son. They looked alike, sounded alike, even had many of the same mannerisms. The similarities ended there, however. From the start Owen was loud, aggressive, and I could see that he'd been the instigator behind this mutiny.

By trade Owen was a salesman. He sold voice recording equipment, and he was darned good at it. For him, as with most salespeople, life was one long negotiation, which he relished. In other words, he was my complete opposite. Here we go, I thought. Yet another shoot-out with a consummate negotiator. When will it end?

Owen began by citing all the things his son had done for Blue Ribbon. He insisted that his son was the main reason Blue Ribbon still existed. I nodded, let him talk himself out, and resisted the urge to make eye contact with Johnson, who sat off to the side. I wondered if they'd rehearsed all this, the way Johnson and I rehearsed my pitch before my last trip to Japan. When Owen finished, when he said that, given the facts, his son obviously should be a full partner in Blue Ribbon, I cleared my throat and conceded that Johnson was a dynamo, that his work had been vital and invaluable. But then I dropped the hammer. "The truth of the matter is, we have forty thousand dollars in sales, and more than that in debt, so there's simply nothing to divvy up here, fellas. We're fighting over slices of a pie that doesn't exist."

Moreover, I told Owen that Bowerman was unwilling to sell any of his stake in Blue Ribbon, and therefore I couldn't sell any of mine. If I did I'd be surrendering majority control of the thing I'd created. That wasn't feasible.

I made my counteroffer. I would give Johnson a fifty-dollar raise. Owen stared. It was a fierce, tough stare, honed during many intense negotiations. He was waiting for me to bend, to up my offer, but for once in my life I had leverage, because I had nothing left to give.

"Take it or leave it" is like four of a kind. Hard to beat.

Finally Owen turned to his son. I think we both knew from the start that Johnson would be the one to settle this, and I saw in Johnson's face that two contrary desires were fighting for his heart. He didn't want to accept my offer. But he didn't want to quit. He loved Blue Ribbon. He needed Blue Ribbon. He saw Blue Ribbon as the one place in the world where he fit, an alternative to the corporate quicksand that had swallowed most of our schoolmates and friends, most of our generation.

He'd complained a million times about my lack of communication, but in fact my laissez-faire management style had fostered him, unleashed him. He wasn't likely to find that kind of autonomy anywhere else. After several seconds he reached out his hand. "Deal," he said. "Deal," I said, shaking it.

We sealed our new agreement with a six-mile run. As I remember, I won.

With Johnson on the East Coast, and Bork taking over his store, I was awash in employees. And then I got a call from Bowerman asking me to add yet *another*. One of his former track guys—Geoff Hollister.

I took Hollister out for a hamburger, and we got along fine, but he cinched the deal by not even flinching when I reached into my pocket and found I didn't have any money to pay for lunch. So I hired him to go around the state selling Tigers, thereby making him Full-Time Employee Number Three.

Soon Bowerman phoned again. He wanted me to hire *another* person. Quadrupling my staff in the span of a few months? Did my old coach think I was General Motors? I might have balked, but then Bowerman said the job candidate's name.

Bob Woodell.

I knew the name, of course. Everyone in Oregon knew the name. Woodell had been a standout on Bowerman's 1965 team. Not quite a star, but a gritty and inspiring competitor. With Oregon defending its second national championship in three years, Woodell had come out of nowhere and won the long jump against vaunted UCLA. I'd been there, I'd watched him do it, and I'd gone away mighty impressed.

The next day there had been a bulletin on TV. An accident at Oregon's Mother's Day Celebrations. Woodell and twenty of his frat brothers were hoisting a float down to the Millrace, a stream that wound through campus. They were trying to flip it over and someone lost their footing. Then someone lost their hold. Someone else let go. Someone screamed, everyone ran. The float collapsed, trapping Woodell underneath, crushing his first lumbar vertebra. There seemed little hope of his walking again.

Bowerman had held a twilight meet at Hayward Field to raise money for Woodell's medical expenses. Now he faced the task of finding something for Woodell to do. At present, he said, the poor guy was sitting around his parents' house in a wheelchair, staring at the walls. Woodell had made tentative inquiries about being Bowerman's assistant coach, but Bowerman said to me: "I just don't think that's going to work, Buck. Maybe he could do something for Blue Ribbon."

I hung up and dialed Woodell. I nearly said how sorry I was about his accident, but I caught myself. I wasn't sure that was the right thing to say. In my mind I ran through another half dozen things, each of which seemed wrong. I'd never been so at a loss for words, and I'd spent half my life tongue-tied. What does one say to a track star who suddenly can't move his legs? I decided to keep it strictly business. I explained that Bowerman had recommended Woodell and said I might have a job for him with my new shoe company. I suggested we get together for lunch. Sure thing, he said.

We met the next day at a sandwich shop in downtown Beaverton, a suburb west of Portland. Woodell drove there himself; he'd already mastered a special car, a Mercury Cougar with hand controls. In fact, he was early. I was fifteen minutes late.

If not for his wheelchair, I don't know that I'd have recognized Woodell when I first walked in. I'd seen him once in person, and several times on TV, but after his many ordeals and surgeries he was shockingly thinner. He'd lost sixty pounds, and his naturally sharp features were now drawn with a much finer pencil. His hair, however, was still jet black, and still grew in remarkably tight curls.

He looked like a bust or frieze of Hermes I'd seen somewhere in the Greek countryside. His eyes were black, too, and they shone with a steeliness, a shrewdness—maybe a sadness. Not unlike Johnson's. Whatever it was, it was mesmerizing, and endearing. I regretted being late.

Lunch was supposed to be a job interview, but the interview part was a formality, we both knew. Men of Oregon take care of their own. Fortunately, loyalty aside, we hit it off. We made each other laugh, mostly about Bowerman. We reminisced about the many ways he tortured runners, ostensibly to instill toughness, like heating a key on a stove and pressing it against their naked flesh in the sauna. We'd both fallen victim. Before long I felt that I'd have given Woodell a job even if he'd been a stranger. Gladly. He was my kind of people. I wasn't certain what Blue Ribbon was, or if it would ever become a thing at all, but whatever it was or might become, I hoped it would have something of this man's spirit.

I offered him a position opening our second retail store, in Eugene, off the campus, at a monthly salary of four hundred dollars. He didn't negotiate, thank goodness. If he'd asked for four thousand a month, I might have found a way.

"Deal?" I said.

"Deal," he said. He reached out, shook my hand.

He still had the strong grip of an athlete.

The waitress brought the check and I told Woodell grandly that lunch was on me. I pulled out my wallet and found that it was empty. I asked Blue Ribbon's Full-Time Employee Number Four if he could float me. Just till payday.

When he wasn't sending me new employees, Bowerman was sending me the results of his latest experiments. In 1966 he'd noticed that the Spring Up's outer sole melted like butter, whereas the midsole remained solid. So he'd urged Onitsuka to take Spring Up's midsole and fuse it with the Limber Up's outer sole, thus creating the ultimate distance training shoe. Now, in 1967, Onitsuka sent us the prototype, and it was astonishing. With its luxurious cushioning and its sleek lines, it looked like the future.

Onitsuka asked what we thought it should be called. Bowerman liked "Aztec," in homage to the 1968 Olympics, which were being held in Mexico City. I liked that, too. Fine, Onitsuka said. The Aztec was born.

And then Adidas threatened to sue. Adidas already had a new shoe named the "Azteca Gold," a track spike they were planning to introduce at the same Olympics. No one had ever heard of it, but that didn't stop Adidas from kicking up a fuss.

Aggravated, I drove up the mountain to Bowerman's house to talk it all over. We sat on the wide porch, looking down at the river. It sparkled that day like a silver shoelace. He took off his ball cap, put it on again, rubbed his face.

"Who was that guy who conquered the Aztecs?" he asked.

"Cortez," I said.

He grunted. "Okay. Let's call it the Cortez."

I was developing an unhealthy contempt for Adidas. Or maybe it was healthy. That one German company had dominated the shoe market for a couple of decades, and they possessed all the arrogance of unchallenged dominance. Of course it's possible that they weren't arrogant at all, that to motivate myself I needed to see them as a monster. In any event, I despised them. I was tired of looking up every day and seeing them far, far ahead. I couldn't bear the thought that it was my fate to do so forever.

The situation put me in mind of Jim Grelle. In high school, Grelle—pronounced *Grella*, or sometimes *Gorilla*—had been the fastest runner in Oregon, and I had been the second-fastest, which meant four years of staring at Grelle's back. Then Grelle and I both went to the University of Oregon, where his tyranny over me continued. By the time I graduated I hoped never again to see Grelle's back. Years later, when Grelle won the 1,500 in Moscow's Lenin Stadium, I was wearing an Army uniform, sitting on a couch in the day room at Fort Lewis. I pumped my fist at the screen, proud of my fellow Oregonian, but I also died a little at the memory of the many times he'd bested me. Now I began to see Adidas as a second Grelle. Chasing them, being legally checked by them, irritated me to no end. It also drove me. Hard.

Once again, in my quixotic effort to overtake a superior opponent, I had Bowerman as my coach. Once again, he was doing everything he could to put me in position to win. I often drew on the memory of his old prerace pep talks, especially when we were up against our blood rival, Oregon State. I would replay Bowerman's epic speeches, hear him telling us that Oregon State wasn't just any opponent. Beating USC and Cal was important, he said, but beating Oregon State was (pause) *different*. Nearly sixty years later it gives me chills to recall his words, his tone. No one could get your blood going like Bowerman, though he never raised his voice. He knew how to speak in subliminal italics, to slyly insert exclamation marks, like hot keys against the flesh.

For extra inspiration I'd sometimes think back to the first time I saw Bowerman walking around the locker room and handing out new shoes. When he came to me, I wasn't even sure I'd made the team. I was a freshman, still unproven, still developing. But he shoved a new pair of spikes straight into my chest. "Knight," he said. That was all. Just my name. Not a syllable more. I looked down at the shoes. They were Oregon green, with yellow stripes, the most breathtaking things I'd ever seen. I cradled them, and later I carried them back to my room and put them gingerly on the top shelf of my bookcase. I remember that I trained my gooseneck desk lamp on them.

They were Adidas, of course.

By the tail end of 1967 Bowerman was inspiring many people besides me. That book he'd been talking about, that silly book about jogging, was done, and out in bookstores. A slight one hundred pages, *Jogging* preached the gospel of physical exercise to a nation that had seldom heard that sermon before, a nation that was collectively lolling on the couch, and somehow the book caught fire. It sold a million copies, sparked a movement, changed the very meaning of the word "running." Before long, thanks to Bowerman and his book, running was no longer just for weirdos. It was no longer a cult. It was almost—cool?

I was happy for him, but also for Blue Ribbon. His best-seller would surely generate publicity and bump our sales. Then I sat down and read the thing. My stomach dropped. In his discussion of proper equipment, Bowerman gave some commonsense advice, followed by some confounding recommendations. Discussing shin splints, or "buck shins," he said the right shoes were important, but almost any shoes would work. "Probably the shoes you wear for gardening, or working around the house, will do just fine."

What?

As for workout clothes, Bowerman told readers that proper clothing "may help the spirit," but added that people shouldn't get hung up on *brands*.

Maybe he thought this was true for the casual jogger, as opposed to the trained athlete, but by God did he need to say so in print? When we were fighting to establish a brand? More to the point, what did this mean about his true opinion of Blue Ribbon—and me? Any shoe would do? If that were true, why in the world were we bothering to sell Tigers? Why were we fiddling around?

Here I was, chasing Adidas, but in a way I was still chasing Bowerman, seeking his approval, and as always it seemed highly unlikely in late 1967 that I'd ever catch either one.

Thanks largely to Bowerman's Cortez, we closed the year in a blaze, meeting our expectation of revenue: eighty-four thousand dollars. I almost looked forward to my next trip to First National. Finally Wallace would back off, loosen the purse strings. Maybe he'd even concede the value of growth.

In the meantime Blue Ribbon had outgrown my apartment. Maybe it's more accurate to say that it had taken over. The place was now the equal of Johnson's bachelor pad. All it needed was a violet light and a baby octopus. I couldn't put it off any longer, I needed a proper office space, so I rented a large room on the east side of town.

It wasn't much. A plain old workspace with a high ceiling and high windows, several of which were broken or stuck open, meaning the room was a constant, brisk fifty degrees. Right next door was a raucous restaurant, the Pink Bucket, and every day at 4:00 p.m., promptly, the jukebox would kick in. The walls were so thin, you could hear the first record drop and feel every thumping note thereafter.

But the rent was cheap. Fifty bucks a month.

When I took Woodell to see it, he allowed it had a certain charm. Woodell needed to like it, because I was transferring him from the Eugene store to this office. He'd shown tremendous skills at the store, a flair for organizing, along with boundless energy, but I could use him better in what I would be calling "the home office." Sure enough, on Day One he came up with a solution to the stuck windows. He brought in one of his old javelins to hook the window latches and push them shut.

We couldn't afford to fix the broken glass in the other windows, so on really cold days we just wore sweaters.

Meanwhile, in the middle of the room I erected a plywood wall, thereby creating warehouse space in the back and retail-office space up front. I was no handyman, and the floor was badly warped, so the wall wasn't close to straight or even. From ten feet away it appeared to undulate. Woodell and I decided that was kind of groovy.

At an office thrift store we bought three battered desks, one for me, one for Woodell, one for "the next person stupid enough to work for us." I also built a corkboard wall, to which I pinned different Tiger models, borrowing some of Johnson's décor ideas in Santa Monica. In a far corner I set up a small sitting area for customers to try on shoes.

One day, at five minutes before 6:00 p.m., a high school kid wandered in. Need some running shoes, he said timidly. Woodell and I looked at each other, looked at the clock. We were beat, but we needed every sale. We talked to the kid about his instep, his stride, his life, and gave him several pairs to try on. He took his time lacing them up, walking around the room, and each pair he declared "not quite right." At 7:00 p.m. he said he'd have to go home and "think about it." He left, and Woodell and I sat amid the mounds of empty boxes and scattered shoes. I looked at him. He looked at me. This is how we're going to build a shoe company?

As I gradually moved my inventory out of my apartment, into my new office, the thought crossed my mind that it might make more sense to give up the apartment altogether, just move into the office, since I'd basically be living there anyway. When I wasn't at Price Waterhouse, making the rent, I'd be at Blue Ribbon, and vice versa. I could shower at the gym.

But I told myself that living in your office is the act of a crazy person.

And then I got a letter from Johnson saying he was living in his new office.

He'd chosen to locate our East Coast office in Wellesley, a tony suburb of Boston. Of course he included a hand-drawn map, and a sketch, and more information than I'd ever need about the history and topography and weather patterns of Wellesley. Also, he told me how he'd come to choose it.

At first he'd considered Long Island, New York. Upon his arrival there he'd rendezvoused with the high school kid who'd alerted him to the East Coast Cowboy's secret machinations.

The kid drove Johnson all over, and Johnson saw enough of Long Island to know that this place wasn't his bag. He left the high school kid, headed north on I-95, and when he hit Wellesley, it just spoke to him. He saw people running along quaint country roads, many of them women, many of them the actress Ali MacGraw look-alikes. Ali MacGraw was Johnson's type. He remembered that Ali MacGraw had attended Wellesley College.

Then he learned, or remembered, that the Boston Marathon route ran right through the town. Sold.

He riffled through his card catalog and found the address of a local customer, another high school track star. He drove to the kid's house, knocked at the door, unannounced. The kid wasn't there, but his parents said Johnson was more than welcome to come in and wait. When the kid got home he found his shoe salesman sitting at the dining room table eating dinner with the whole family. The next day, after they went for a run, Johnson got from the kid a list of names—local coaches, potential customers, likely contacts—and a list of what neighborhoods he might like. Within days he'd found and rented a little house behind a funeral parlor. Claiming it in the name of Blue Ribbon, he also made it his home. He wanted me to go halfsies on the two-hundred-dollar rent.

In a PS he said I should buy him furniture also.

I didn't answer.

1968

I was putting in six days a week at Price Waterhouse, spending early mornings and late night and all weekends and vacations at Blue Ribbon. No friends, no exercise, no social life—and wholly content. My life was out of balance, sure, but I didn't care. In fact, I wanted even more imbalance. Or a different kind of imbalance.

I wanted to dedicate every minute of every day to Blue Ribbon. I'd never been a multitasker, and I didn't see any reason to start now. I wanted to be present, always. I wanted to focus constantly on the one task that really mattered. If my life was to be all work and no play, I wanted my work to be play. I wanted to quit Price Waterhouse. Not that I hated it; it just wasn't me.

I wanted what everyone wants. To be me, full-time.

But it wasn't possible. Blue Ribbon simply couldn't support me. Though the company was on track to double sales for a fifth straight year, it still couldn't justify a salary for its cofounder. So I decided to compromise, find a different day job, one that would pay my bills but require fewer hours, leaving me more time for my passion.

The only job I could think of that fit this criterion was teaching. I applied to Portland State University and got a job as an assistant professor, at seven hundred dollars a month.

I should have been delighted to quit Price Waterhouse, but I'd learned a lot there, and I was sad about leaving Hayes. "I'm going to focus on my shoe thing," I told him. Hayes frowned, grumbled something about missing me, or admiring me.

I asked what he was going to do. He said he was going to ride it out at Price Waterhouse. Lose fifty pounds, make partner, that was his plan. I wished him luck.

As part of my formal severing, I had to go in and talk to the boss, a senior partner with the Dickensian name of Curly Leclerc. He was polite, even-handed, smooth, playing a one-act drama he'd played a hundred times—the exit interview. He asked what I was going to do instead of working for one of the finest accounting firms in the world. I said that I'd started my own business and was hoping it might take off, and in the meantime I was going to teach accounting.

He stared. I'd gone off script. Way off. "Why the hell would you do something like that?"

Lastly, the really difficult exit interview. I told my father. He, too, stared. Bad enough I was still messing around with shoes, he said, but now . . . *this*. Teaching wasn't respectable. Teaching at Portland State was downright disrespectable. "What am I going to tell my friends?" he asked.

The university assigned me four accounting classes, including Accounting 101. I spent a few hours prepping, reviewing basic concepts, and as fall arrived the balance of my life shifted just as I'd planned. I still didn't have all the time I wanted or needed for Blue Ribbon, but I had more. I was following a path that felt like my path, and though I wasn't sure where it would lead, I was ready to find out.

So I was beaming with hope on that first day of the semester, in early September 1967. My students, however, were not. Slowly they filed into the classroom, each one radiating boredom and hostility. For the next hour they were to be confined in this stifling cage, force-fed some of the driest concepts ever devised, and I was to blame, which made me the target of their resentment. They eyed me, frowned. A few scowled.

I empathized. But I wasn't going to let them rattle me. Standing at the lectern in my black suit and skinny gray tie, I remained calm, for the most part. I was always somewhat restless, somewhat twitchy, and in those days I had several nervous tics—like wrapping rubber bands around my wrist and playing with them, snapping them against my skin. I might have snapped them extra fast, extra hard, as I saw the students slump into the room like prisoners on a chain gang.

Suddenly, sweeping lightly into the classroom and taking a seat in the front row was a striking young woman. She had long golden hair that brushed her shoulders, and matching golden hoop earrings that also brushed her shoulders. I looked at her, and she looked at me. Bright blue eyes set off by dramatic black eyeliner.

I thought of Cleopatra. I thought of Julie Christie. I thought: Jeez, Julie Christie's kid sister has just enrolled in my accounting class.

I wondered how old she was. She couldn't yet be twenty, I guessed, snapping my rubber bands against my wrist, snapping, snapping, and staring, then pretending not to stare. She was hard to look away from. And hard to figure. So young, and yet so worldly. Those earrings—they were strictly hippie, and yet that eye makeup was très chic. Who was this girl? And how was I going to concentrate on teaching with her in the front row?

I called roll. I can still remember the names. "Mr. Trujillo?"

"Here."

"Mr. Peterson?"

"Here."

"Mr. Jameson?"

"Here."

"Miss Parks?"

"Here," said Julie Christie's kid sister, softly.

I looked up, gave a half smile. She gave a half smile. I penciled a shaky check next to her full name: Penelope Parks. Penelope, like the faithful wife of world-traveling Odysseus.

Present and accounted for.

I decided to employ the Socratic method. I was emulating the Oregon and Stanford professors whose classes I'd enjoyed most, I guess. And I was still under the spell of all things Greek, still enchanted by my day at the Acropolis. But maybe, by asking questions rather than lecturing, I was also trying to deflect attention from myself, force students to participate. Especially certain pretty students.

"Okay, class," I said, "you buy three virtually identical widgets for one dollar, two dollars, and three dollars, respectively. You sell one for five dollars. What's the *cost* of that sold widget? And what's the gross profit on the sale?"

Several hands went up. None, alas, was Miss Parks's. She was looking down. Shier than the professor, apparently. I was forced to call on Mr. Trujillo, and then Mr. Peterson.

"Okay," I said. "Now, Mr. Trujillo recorded his inventory on a FIFO basis and made a gross profit of four dollars. Mr. Peterson used LIFO and had a gross profit of two dollars. So . . . who has the better business?"

A spirited discussion followed, involving nearly everybody

but Miss Parks. I looked at her. And looked. She didn't speak. She didn't look up. Maybe she wasn't shy, I thought. Maybe she just wasn't very bright. How sad if she'd have to drop the class. Or if I'd have to flunk her.

Early on, I drummed into my students the primary principle of all accounting: Assets equal liabilities plus equity. This foundational equation, I said, must always, always be in balance. Accounting is problem solving, I said, and most problems boil down to some imbalance in this equation. To solve, therefore, get it balanced. I felt a little hypocritical saying this, since my company had an out-of-whack liabilities-to-equity ratio of ninety to ten. More than once I winced to think what Wallace would say if he could sit in on one of my classes. My students apparently weren't any more capable than I of balancing this equation. Their homework papers were dreadful. That is, with the exception of Miss Parks! She aced the first assignment. With the next and the next she established herself as the top student in the class. And she didn't just get every answer right. Her penmanship was exquisite. Like Japanese calligraphy. A girl that looked like that—*and* whip smart?

She went on to record the highest grade in the class on the midterm. I don't know who was happier, Miss Parks or Mr. Knight.

Not long after I handed back the tests she lingered at my desk, asking if she could have a word. Of course, I said, reaching for my wrist rubber bands, giving them a series of vehement snaps. She asked if I might consider being her adviser. I was taken back. "Oh," I said. "Oh. I'd be honored."

Then I blurted: "How would *you* . . . like . . . a job?"

"A what?"

"I've got this little shoe company . . . uh . . . on the side. And it needs some bookkeeping help."

She was holding her textbooks against her chest. She adjusted them and fluttered her eyelashes. "Oh," she said. "Oh. Well. Okay. That sounds . . . fun."

I offered to pay her two dollars an hour. She nodded. Deal.

Days later she arrived at the office. Woodell and I gave her the third desk. She sat, placed her palms on the desktop, looked around the room. "What do you want me to do?" she asked.

Woodell handed her a list of things—typing, bookkeeping, scheduling, stocking, filing invoices—and told her to pick one or two each day and have at it.

But she didn't pick. She did them all. Quickly, and with ease. Inside a week neither Woodell nor I could remember how we'd ever gotten along without her.

It wasn't just the quality of Miss Parks's work that we found so valuable. It was the blithe spirit in which she did it. From Day One, she was all in. She grasped what we were trying to do, what we were trying to build here. She felt that Blue

Ribbon was unique, that it might become something special, and she wanted to do what she could to help. Which proved to be a lot.

She had a remarkable way with people, especially the sales reps we were continuing to hire. Whenever they came into the office, Miss Parks would size them up, fast, and either charm them or put them in their place, depending on what was called for. Though shy, she could be wry, funny, and the sales reps—that is, the ones she liked—often left laughing, looking back over their shoulders, wondering what just hit them.

The impact of Miss Parks was most apparent in Woodell. He was going through a bad time just then. His body was fighting the wheelchair, resisting its life imprisonment. He was plagued by maladies related to sitting motionless, and often he'd be out sick for weeks at a time. But when he was in the office, when he was sitting alongside Miss Parks, she brought the color back to his cheeks. She had a healing effect on him, and seeing this had a bewitching effect on me.

Most days I surprised myself, offering eagerly to run across the street to get lunch for Miss Parks and Woodell. This was the kind of thing we might have asked Miss Parks to do, but day after day I volunteered. Was it chivalry? Devilry? What was happening to me? I didn't recognize myself.

And yet some things never change. My head was so full of debits and credits, and shoes, shoes, shoes, that I rarely got the lunch orders right. Miss Parks never complained. Nor did Woodell. Invariably I'd hand each of them a brown paper bag and they'd exchange a knowing glance. "Can't wait to see what I'm eating for lunch today," Woodell would mutter. Miss Parks would put a hand over her mouth, concealing a smile.

Miss Parks saw my bewitchment, I think. There were several long looks between us, several meaningfully awkward pauses. I recall one burst of particularly nervous laughter, one portentous silence. I remember one long moment of eye contact that kept me awake that night.

Then it happened. On a cold afternoon in late November, when Miss Parks wasn't in the office, I was walking toward the back of the office and noticed her desk drawer open. I stopped to close it and inside I saw . . . a stack of checks? All her paychecks—uncashed.

This wasn't a job to her. This was something else. And so perhaps . . . was I? Maybe?

Maybe.

(Later, I learned Woodell was doing the same thing.)

That Thanksgiving a record cold spell hit Portland. The breeze coming through the holes in the office windows was now a fierce arctic wind. At times the gusts were so strong, papers flew from the desktops, shoelaces on the samples fluttered. The office was intolerable, but we couldn't afford to fix the windows, and we couldn't shut down. So Woodell and I moved to my apartment, and Miss Parks joined us there each afternoon.

One day, after Woodell had gone home, neither Miss Parks nor I said much. At quitting time I walked her out to the elevator. I pressed the down button. We both smiled tensely. I pressed down again. We both stared at the light above the elevator doors. I cleared my throat. "Miss Parks," I said, "would you like to, uhh . . . maybe go out on Friday night?"

Those Cleopatra eyes. They doubled in size. "Me?"

"I don't see anyone else here," I said.

Ping. The elevator doors slid open.

"Oh," she said, looking down at her feet. "Well. Okay. Okay." She hurried onto the elevator, and as the doors closed she never lifted her gaze from her shoes.

I took her to the Oregon Zoo. I don't know why. I guess I thought walking around and gazing at animals would be a low-key way of getting to know each other. Also, Burmese pythons, Nigerian goats, African crocodiles, they would give me ample opportunities to impress her with tales of my travels. I felt the need to brag about seeing the pyramids, the Temple of Nike. I also told her about falling ill in Calcutta. I'd never described that scary moment, in detail, to anyone. I didn't know why I was telling Miss Parks, except that Calcutta had been one of the loneliest moments of my life, and I felt very unlonely just then.

I confessed that Blue Ribbon was tenuous. The whole

thing might go bust any day, but I still couldn't see myself doing anything else. My little shoe company was a living, breathing thing, I said, which I'd created from nothing. I'd breathed it into life, nurtured it through illness, brought it back several times from the dead, and now I wanted, needed, to see it stand on its own feet and go out into the world. "Does that make sense?" I said.

"Mm-hmm," she said.

We strolled past the lions and tigers. I told her that I flat-out didn't want to work for someone else. I wanted to build something that was my own, something I could point to and say: I made that. It was the only way I saw to make life meaningful.

She nodded. Like basic accounting principles, she grasped it all intuitively, right away.

I asked if she was seeing anyone. She confessed that she was. But the boy—well, she said, he was just a boy. All the boys she dated, she said, were just that—boys. They talked about sports and cars. (I was smart enough not to confess that I loved both.) "But you," she said, "you've seen the world. And now you're putting everything on the line to create this company ..."

Her voice trailed off. I stood up straighter. We said goodbye to the lions and tigers.

For our second date we walked over to Jade West, a Chinese restaurant across the street from the office. Over Mongolian beef and garlic chicken she told me her story. She still lived at home, and loved her family very much, but there were challenges. Her father was an admiralty lawyer, which struck me as a good job. Their house certainly sounded bigger and better than the one in which I'd grown up. But five kids, she hinted, was a strain. Money was a constant issue. A certain amount of rationing was standard operating procedure. There was never enough; staples, like toilet paper, were always in low supply. It was a home marked by *insecurity*. She did *not* like insecurity. She preferred security. She said it again. *Security*. That's why she'd been drawn to accounting. It seemed solid, dependable, safe, a line of work she could always rely on.

I asked how she'd happened to choose Portland State. She said she'd started out at Oregon State.

"Oh," I said, as if she'd confessed to doing time in prison.

She laughed. "If it's any consolation, I hated it." In particular, she couldn't abide the school's requirement that every student take at least one class in public speaking. She was far too shy.

"I understand, Miss Parks."

"Call me Penny."

After dinner I drove her home and met her parents. "Mom, Dad, this is Mr. Knight."

"Pleased to meet you," I said, shaking their hands.

We all stared at each other. Then the walls. Then the floor. Lovely weather we're having, isn't it?

"Well," I said, tapping my watch, snapping my rubber bands, "it's late, I'd better be going."

Her mother looked at a clock on the wall. "It's only nine o'clock," she said. "Some hot date."

Just after our second date Penny went with her parents to Hawaii for Christmas. She sent me a postcard, and I took this as a good sign. When she returned, her first day back at the office, I asked her again to dinner. It was early January 1968, a bitterly cold night. Again we went to Jade West, but this time I met her there, and I was quite late, arriving from my Eagle Scout review board, for which she gave me much grief. "Eagle Scout? You?"

I took this as another good sign. She felt comfortable enough to tease me.

At some point during that third date, I noticed we were both much more at ease. It felt nice. The ease continued, and over the next few weeks deepened. We developed a rapport, a feel for each other, a knack for communicating nonverbally. As only two shy people can. When she was feeling shy, or uncomfortable, I sensed it, and either gave her space or tried to draw her out, depending. When I was spaced out, embroiled in some internal debate with myself about the business, she knew whether to tap me lightly on the shoulder or wait patiently for me to reemerge.

Time worked its magic. By February, around my thirtieth birthday, she was spending every minute of her free time at Blue Ribbon, and we spent every evening together too. At some point she stopped calling me Mr. Knight.

Inevitably, I brought her home to meet my family. We all sat around the dining room table, eating Mom's pot roast, washing it down with cold milk, pretending it wasn't awkward. Penny was the second girl I'd ever brought home, and though she didn't have the wild charisma of Sarah, what she had was better. Her charm was real, unrehearsed, and though the Knights seemed to like it, they were still the Knights. My mother said nothing; my sisters tried in vain to be a bridge to my mother and father; my father asked a series of probing, thoughtful questions about Penny's background and upbringing, which made him sound like a cross between a loan officer and a homicide detective. Penny told me later that the atmosphere was the exact opposite of her house, where dinner was a free-for-all, everyone laughing and talking over one another, dogs barking and TVs blaring in the background. I assured her that no one would have suspected she felt out of her element.

Next she brought me home, and I saw the truth of everything she'd told me. Her house *was* the opposite. Though much grander than Chateau Knight, it was a mess. The carpets were stained from all the animals—a German shepherd, a monkey, a cat, several white rats, an ill-tempered goose. And chaos was the rule. Besides the Parks clan, and their arkful of pets, it was a hangout for all the stray kids in the neighborhood.

I tried my best to be charming, but I couldn't seem to connect with anyone, human or otherwise. Slowly, painstakingly, I made inroads with Penny's mother, Dot. She reminded me of Auntie Mame—zany, madcap, eternally young. In many ways she was a permanent teenager, resisting her role as matriarch. It struck me that she was more like a sister to Penny than a mother.

Penny and I spent every waking moment together for months. At some point I raised the subject of our future. I was leaving the next day for a long and vital trip to Japan, to cement my relationship with Onitsuka, I hoped. When I returned, later that summer, we couldn't keep "dating," I told her. Portland State frowned on teacher-student relationships. We'd have to do something to formalize our relationship, to set it above reproach. Meaning, marriage. "Can you handle arranging a wedding by yourself while I'm gone?" I said.

"Yes," she said.

There was very little discussion, or suspense, or emotion. There was no negotiation. It all felt like a foregone conclusion.

I kept saying to myself, over and over, I'm engaged, I'm engaged. But it didn't sink in. Later, when we went to Zell Bros. Jewelers and picked out an engagement ring with an emerald stone, it started to feel real. The stone and setting cost five hundred dollars—*that* was *very* real. But I never once felt nervous, never asked myself with that typical male remorse, Oh, God, what have I done? The months of dating and getting to know Penny had been the happiest of my life, and now I would have the chance to perpetuate that happiness. That's how I saw it. Basic as Accounting 101. Assets equal liabilities plus equity.

Not until I left for Japan, not until I kissed my fiancée good-bye and promised to write as soon as I got there, did the full reality, with all its dimensions and contours, hit me. I had more than a fiancée. I had a partner. In the past I'd told myself Bowerman was my partner, and to some extent Johnson. But this thing with Penny was unique, unprecedented. This alliance was life-altering. It still didn't make me nervous, it just made me more mindful. I'd never before said good-bye to a true partner, and it felt massively different. Imagine that, I thought. The single easiest way to find out how you feel about someone. Say good-bye.

For once, my former contact at Onitsuka was still my contact. Kitami was still there. He hadn't been replaced. He hadn't been reassigned. On the contrary, his role with the company was more secure, judging by his demeanor. He seemed easier, more self-assured.

He welcomed me like one of the family, said he was delighted with Blue Ribbon's performance, and with our East

Coast office, which was thriving under Johnson. "Now let us work on how we can capture the U.S. market," he said.

"I like the sound of that," I said.

In my briefcase I was carrying new shoe designs from both Bowerman and Johnson, including one they'd teamed up on, a shoe we were calling the Boston. It had an innovative full-length midsole cushion. Kitami put the designs on the wall and studied them closely. He held his chin in one hand. He liked them, he said. "Like very very much," he said, slapping me on the back.

We met many times over the course of the next several weeks, and each time I sensed from Kitami an almost brotherly vibe. One afternoon he mentioned that his export department was having its annual picnic in a few days. "You come!" he said.

"Me?" I said.

"Yes, yes," he said, "you are honorary member of export department."

The picnic was on Awaji, a tiny island off Kobe. We took a small boat to get there, and when we arrived we saw long tables set up along the beach, each one covered with platters of seafood and bowls of noodles and rice. Beside the tables were tubs filled with cold bottles of soda and beer. Everyone was wearing bathing suits and sunglasses and laughing. People I'd only known in a reserved, corporate setting were being silly and carefree.

Late in the day there were competitions. Team-building exercises like potato sack relays and footraces along the surf. I showed off my speed, and everyone bowed to me as I crossed the finish line first. Everyone agreed that Skinny Gaijin was very fast.

I was picking up the language, slowly. I knew the Japanese word for shoe: *gutzu*. I knew the Japanese word for revenue: *shunyu*. I knew how to ask the time, and directions, and I learned a phrase I used often: *Watakushi domo no kaisha ni tsuite no joh hou des*. Here is some information about my company.

Toward the end of the picnic I sat on the sand and looked out across the Pacific Ocean. I was living two separate lives, both wonderful, both merging. Back home I was part of a team, me and Woodell and Johnson—and now Penny. Here in Japan I was part of a team, me and Kitami and all the good people of Onitsuka. By nature I was a loner, but since childhood I'd thrived in team sports. My psyche was in true harmony when I had a mix of alone time and team time. Exactly what I had now.

Also, I was doing business with a country I'd come to love. Gone was the initial fear. I connected with the shyness of the Japanese people, with the simplicity of their culture and products and arts. I liked that they tried to add beauty to every part of life, from the tea ceremony to the commode. I liked that the radio announced each day exactly which cherry trees, on which corner, were blossoming, and how much.

My reverie was interrupted when a man named Fujimoto sat beside me. Fiftyish, slouch-shouldered, he had a gloomy air that seemed more than middle-age melancholy. Like a Japanese

Charlie Brown. And yet I could see that he was making a concerted effort to extend himself, to be cheerful toward me. He forced a big smile and told me that he loved America, that he longed to live there. I told him that I'd just been thinking how much I loved Japan. "Maybe we should trade places," I said.

He smiled ruefully. "Anytime."

I complimented his English. He said he'd learned it from the American servicemen. "Funny," I said, "the first things I learned about Japanese culture, I learned from two ex-servicemen."

The first words his servicemen taught him, he said, were, "Kiss my butt!" We had a good laugh about that.

I asked where he lived and his smile disappeared. "Months ago," he said, "I lose my home. Typhoon Billie." The storm had completely wiped away the Japanese islands of Honshu and Kyushu, along with two thousand houses. "Mine," Fujimoto said, "was one of houses."

"I'm very sorry," I said.

He nodded, looked at the water. He'd started over, he said. As the Japanese do. The one thing he hadn't been able to replace, unfortunately, was his bicycle. In the 1960s bicycles were exorbitantly expensive in Japan.

Kitami now joined us. I noticed that Fujimoto got up right away and walked off.

I mentioned to Kitami that Fujimoto had learned his English from servicemen, and Kitami said with pride that he'd learned his English all by himself, from a record. I congratulated him, and said I hoped one day to be as fluent in Japanese as he was in English. Then I mentioned that I was getting married soon. I told him a bit about Penny, and he congratulated me and wished me luck. "When is wedding?" he asked.

"September," I said.

"Ah," he said, "I will be in America one month after, when Mr. Onitsuka and I attend Olympics in Mexico City. We might visit Los Angeles."

He invited me to fly down, have dinner with them. I said I'd be delighted.

The next day I returned to the United States, and one of the first things I did after landing was put fifty dollars in an envelope and airmail it to Fujimoto. On the card I wrote: *For a new bicycle, my friend.*

Weeks later an envelope arrived from Fujimoto. My fifty dollars, folded inside a note explaining that he'd asked his superiors if he could keep the money, and they'd said no.

There was a PS: *If you send my house, I can keep.* So I did.

And thus another life-altering partnership was born.

On September 13, 1968, Penny and I exchanged our vows before two hundred people at St. Mark's Episcopal Church in downtown Portland, at the same altar where Penny's parents had been married. It was one year, nearly to the day, after Miss

Parks had first walked into my classroom. She was again in the front row, of a sort, only this time I was standing beside her. And she was now Mrs. Knight.

My best man was Cousin Houser. My lawyer, my wing-man. The other groomsmen were Penny's two brothers, plus a friend from business school, and Cale, who told me moments before the ceremony, "Second time I've seen you this nervous." We laughed, and reminisced, for the millionth time, about that day at Stanford when I'd given my presentation to my entrepreneurship class. Today, I thought, is similar. Once again I'm telling a roomful of people that something is possible, that something can be successful, when in fact I don't really know. I'm speaking from theory, faith, and bluster, like every groom. And every bride. It would be up to me and Penny to prove the truth of what we said that day.

The reception was at the Portland Garden Club, where society ladies gathered on summer nights to drink daiquiris and trade gossip. The night was warm. The skies threatened rain, but never opened. I danced with Penny. I danced with Dot. I danced with my mother. Before midnight Penny and I said good-bye to all and jumped into my brand-new car, a racy black Cougar. I sped us to the coast, two hours away, where we planned to spend the weekend at her parents' beach house.

Dot called every half hour.

1969

Suddenly, a whole new cast of characters was wandering in and out of the office. Rising sales enabled me to hire more and more reps. Most were ex-runners, and eccentrics, as only ex-runners can be. But when it came to selling they were all business. Because they were inspired by what we were trying to do, and because they worked solely on commission (two dollars a pair), they were burning up the roads, hitting every high school and college track meet within a thousand-mile radius, and their extraordinary efforts were boosting our numbers even more.

We'd posted $150,000 in sales in 1968, and in 1969 we were on our way to just under $300,000. Though Wallace was still breathing down my neck, hassling me to slow down and moaning about my lack of equity, I decided that Blue Ribbon was doing well enough to justify a salary for its founder. Right before my thirty-first birthday I made the bold move. I quit Portland State and went full-time at my company, paying myself a fairly generous eighteen thousand dollars a year.

Above all, I told myself, the best reason for leaving Portland State was that I'd already gotten more out of the school—Penny—than I'd ever hoped. I got something else, too; I just didn't know it at the time. Nor did I dream how valuable it would prove to be.

In my last week on campus, walking through the halls, I noticed a group of young women standing around an easel. One of them was daubing at a large canvas, and just as I passed I heard her lamenting that she couldn't afford to take a class on oil painting. I stopped, admired the canvas. "My company could use an artist," I said.

"What?" she said.

"My company needs someone to do some advertising. Would you like to make some extra money?"

I still didn't see any bang-for-the-buck in advertising, but I was starting to accept that I could no longer ignore it. The Standard Insurance Company had just run a full-page ad in the *Wall Street Journal*, touting Blue Ribbon as one of the dynamic young companies among its clients. The ad featured a photo of Bowerman and me . . . staring at a shoe. Not as if we were shoe innovators; more as if we'd never seen a shoe before. We looked like morons. It was embarrassing.

In some of our ads the model was none other than Johnson. See Johnson rocking a blue tracksuit. See Johnson waving a javelin. When it came to advertising, our approach was primitive and slapdash. We were making it up as we went along, learning on the fly, and it showed. In one ad—for the Tiger marathon flat, I think—we referred to the new fabric as "swooshfiber." To this day none of us remembers who first came up with the word, or what it meant. But it sounded good.

People were telling me constantly that advertising was important, that advertising was the next wave. I always rolled my eyes. But if icky photos and made-up words—and Johnson, posed seductively on a couch—were slipping into our ads, I needed to start paying more attention.

"I'll give you two bucks an hour," I told this starving artist in the hallway at Portland State.

"To do what?" she asked.

"Design print ads," I said, "do some lettering, logos, maybe a few charts and graphs for presentations."

It didn't sound like much of a gig. But the poor kid was desperate.

She wrote her name on a piece of paper. Carolyn Davidson. And her number. I shoved it in my pocket and forgot all about it.

Hiring sales reps and graphic artists showed great optimism, and I didn't consider myself an optimist by nature. Not that I was a pessimist. I generally tried to hover between the two, committing to neither. But as 1969 approached, I found myself staring into space and thinking the future might be bright. After a good night's sleep, after a hearty breakfast, I could see plenty of reason for hope. Aside from our robust and rising sales numbers, Onitsuka would soon be bringing out several exciting new models, including the Obori, which featured a feather-light nylon upper. Also, the Marathon, another nylon, with lines sleek as a Karmann Ghia. These shoes will sell themselves, I told Woodell many times, hanging them on the corkboard.

Also, Bowerman was back from Mexico City, where he'd been an assistant coach on the U.S. Olympic team, meaning he'd played a pivotal role in the United States winning more gold medals than any team, from any nation, ever. My partner was more than famous; he was legendary.

I phoned Bowerman, eager to get his overall thoughts on the Games, and particularly on the moment for which they would forever be remembered, the protest of John Carlos and Tommie Smith. Standing on the podium during the playing of "The Star-Spangled Banner," both men had bowed their heads and raised black-gloved fists, a shocking gesture, meant to call attention to racism, poverty, human rights abuses. They were still being condemned for it. But Bowerman, as I fully expected, supported them. Bowerman supported all runners.

Carlos and Smith were shoeless during the protest; they'd conspicuously removed their Pumas and left them on the stands. I told Bowerman I couldn't decide if this had been a good thing or a bad thing for Puma. Was all publicity really good publicity? Was publicity like advertising? A chimera?

Bowerman chuckled and said he wasn't sure.

He told me about the scandalous behavior of Puma and Adidas throughout the Games. The world's two biggest athletic shoe companies—run by two German brothers who despised each other—had chased each other like Keystone Kops around the Olympic Village, jockeying for all the athletes. Huge sums of cash, often stuffed in running shoes or manila envelopes, were passed around. One of Puma's sales reps even got thrown in jail. (There were rumors that Adidas had framed him.) He was married to a female sprinter, and Bowerman joked that he'd only married her to secure her endorsement.

Worse, it didn't stop at mere payouts. Puma had smuggled truckloads of shoes into Mexico City, while Adidas cleverly managed to evade Mexico's stiff import tariffs. I heard through the grapevine they did it by making a nominal number of shoes at a factory in Guadalajara.

Bowerman and I didn't feel morally offended; we felt left out. Blue Ribbon had no money for payouts, and therefore no presence at the Games.

We'd had one meager booth in the Olympic Village, and

one guy working it—Bork. I didn't know if Bork had been sitting there reading comic books or just hadn't been able to compete with the massive presence of Adidas and Puma, but either way his booth generated zero business, zero buzz. No one stopped by.

Actually, one person did stop by. Bill Toomey, a brilliant American decathlete, asked for some Tigers, so he could show the world that he couldn't be bought. But Bork didn't have his size. Nor the right shoes for any of his events.

Plenty of athletes were training in Tigers, Bowerman reported. We just didn't have anybody actually *competing* in them. Part of the reason was quality; Tigers just weren't good enough yet. The main reason, however, was money. We had not a penny for endorsement deals.

"We're not broke," I told Bowerman, "we just don't have any money."

He grunted. "Either way," he said, "wouldn't it be wonderful to be able to *pay* athletes? Legally?"

Lastly, Bowerman told me he'd bumped into Kitami at the Games. He didn't much care for the man. "Doesn't know a damn thing about shoes," Bowerman grumbled. "And he's a little too slick. Little too full of himself."

I was starting to have the same inklings. I'd gotten a sense from Kitami's last few wires and letters that he might not be the man he'd seemed, and that he wasn't the fan of Blue Ribbon he'd appeared to be when I was last in Japan. I had a bad feeling in my bones. Maybe he was getting ready to jack up our prices. I mentioned this to Bowerman, and told him I was taking measures to protect us. Before hanging up I boasted that, though I didn't have enough cash or cachet to pay athletes, I did have enough to buy someone at Onitsuka. I had a man on the inside, I said, a man acting as my eyes and ears and keeping tabs on Kitami.

I sent out a memo saying as much to all Blue Ribbon employees. (By now we had around forty.) Though I'd fallen in love with Japanese culture—I kept my souvenir samurai sword beside my desk—I also warned them that Japanese business practices were thoroughly perplexing. In Japan you couldn't predict what either your competition or your partner might do. I'd given up trying. Instead, I wrote, *I've taken what I think is a big step to keep us informed. I've hired a spy. He works full-time in the Onitsuka export department. Without going into a lengthy discussion of why I will just tell you that I feel he is trustworthy.*

This spy may seem somewhat unethical to you, but the spy system is ingrained and completely accepted in Japanese business circles. They actually have schools for industrial spies, much as we have schools for typists and stenographers.

I can't imagine what made me use the word "spy" so wantonly, so boldly, other than the fact that James Bond was all the rage just then. Nor can I understand why, when I was revealing so much, I didn't reveal the spy's name. It was Fujimoto, whose bicycle I'd replaced.

I think I must have known, on some level, that the memo was a mistake, a terribly stupid thing to do. And that I would live to regret it. I *think* I knew. But I often found myself as perplexing as Japanese business practices.

Kitami and Mr. Onitsuka both attended the Games in Mexico City, and afterward they both flew to Los Angeles. I flew down from Oregon to meet them for dinner at a Japanese restaurant in Santa Monica. I was late, of course, and by the time I arrived they were like schoolboys on holiday: Each was wearing a souvenir sombrero, loudly woohooing.

I tried hard to mirror their festive mood. I helped them finish off several platters of sushi, and generally bonded with them both. At my hotel that night I went to bed thinking, hoping, I'd been paranoid about Kitami.

The next morning we all flew to Portland so they could meet the gang at Blue Ribbon. I realized that in my letters to Onitsuka, not to mention my conversations with them, I might have overplayed the grandeur of our "worldwide headquarters." Sure enough, I saw Kitami's face drop as he walked in. I also saw Mr. Onitsuka looking around, bewildered. I hastened to apologize. "It may look small," I said, laughing tightly, "but we do a lot of business out of this room!"

They looked at the broken windows, the javelin window closer, the wavy plywood room divider. They looked at Woodell in his wheelchair. They felt the walls vibrating from the Pink Bucket jukebox. They looked at each other, dubious. I told myself: Whelp, it's all over.

Sensing my embarrassment, Mr. Onitsuka put a reassuring hand on my shoulder. "It is . . . most charming," he said.

On the far wall Woodell had hung a large, handsome map of the United States, and he'd put a red pushpin everywhere we'd sold a pair of Tigers in the last five years. The map was covered with red pushpins. For one merciful moment it diverted attention from our office space. Then Kitami pointed at eastern Montana. "No pins," he said. "Obviously salesman here not doing job."

Days went swooshing by. I was trying to build a company and a marriage. Penny and I were learning to live together, learning to meld our personalities and idiosyncrasies, though we agreed that she was the one with all the personality and I was the idiosyncratic one. Therefore, it was she who had more to learn.

Leaning back in my recliner each night, staring at the ceiling, I tried to settle myself. I told myself: Life is growth. You grow or you die.

•   •   •

Once we found out Penny was pregnant, we found a house in Beaverton. Small, only sixteen hundred square feet, but it had an acre of land around it, and a little horse corral, and a pool. There was also a huge pine tree in the front and a Japanese bamboo out back. I loved it. More, I recognized it. When I was growing up my sisters asked me several times what my dream house would look like, and one day they handed me a charcoal pencil and a pad and made me draw it. After Penny and I moved in, my sisters dug out the old charcoal sketch. It was an exact picture of the Beaverton house.

The price was thirty-four thousand dollars, and I popped my shirt buttons to discover that I had 20 percent of that in savings. On the other hand, I'd pledged those savings against my many loans at First National. So I went down to talk to Harry White. I need the savings for a down payment on a house, I said—but I'll pledge the house.

"Okay," he said. "On this one we don't have to consult Wallace."

That night I told Penny that if Blue Ribbon failed we'd lose the house. She put a hand on her stomach and sat down. This was the kind of *insecurity* she'd always vowed to avoid. Okay, she kept saying, okaaaay.

With so much at stake, she felt compelled to keep working for Blue Ribbon, right through her pregnancy. She would sacrifice everything to Blue Ribbon, even her deeply held goal of graduating from college. And when she wasn't physically in the office, she would run a mail-order business out of the new house. In 1969 alone, despite morning sickness, swollen ankles, weight gain, and constant fatigue, Penny got out fifteen hundred orders. Some of the orders were nothing more than crude tracings of a human foot, sent in by customers in far-flung places, but Penny didn't care. She dutifully matched the tracing to the correct shoe and filled the order. Every sale counted.

At the same time that my family outgrew its home, so did my business. One room beside the Pink Bucket could no longer contain us. Also, Woodell and I were tired of shouting to be heard above that jukebox. So each night after work we'd go out for cheeseburgers, then drive around looking at office space.

Logistically, it was a nightmare. Woodell had to drive, because his wheelchair wouldn't fit in my Cougar, and I always felt guilty and uncomfortable, being chauffeured by a man with so many limitations. I also felt crazed with nerves, because many of the offices we looked at were up a flight of stairs. Or several flights. This meant I'd have to wheel Woodell up and down.

At such moments I was reminded, painfully, of his reality. During a typical workday, Woodell was so positive, so energetic, it was easy to forget. But wheeling him, maneuvering him, upstairs, downstairs, I was repeatedly struck by how delicate, how helpless he could be. I'd pray under my breath. *Please don't let me drop him. Please don't let me drop him.* Woodell, hearing me, would tense up, and his tension would make me more nervous. "Relax," I'd say, "I haven't lost a patient yet—haha!"

No matter what happened, he'd never lose his composure. Even at his most vulnerable, with me balancing him precariously at the top of some dark flight of stairs, he'd never lose touch with his essential philosophy: *Don't you dare feel sorry for me. I'm here to kill you.*

(The first time I ever sent him to a trade show, the airline lost his wheelchair. And when they found it, the frame was bent like a pretzel. No problem. In his mutilated chair, Woodell attended the show, ticked off every item on his to-do list, and came home with an ear-to-ear mission-accomplished smile on his face.)

At the end of each night's search for new office space, Woodell and I would always have a big belly laugh about the whole debacle. Before parting we'd often play a game. I'd bring out a stopwatch and we'd see how fast Woodell could fold up his wheelchair and get it and himself into his car. As a former track star, he loved the challenge of a stopwatch, of trying to beat his personal best. (His record was forty-four seconds.) We both cherished those nights, the silliness, the sense of shared mission, and we mutually ranked them among the solid gold memories of our young lives.

Woodell and I were very different, and yet our friendship was based on a selfsame approach to work. Each of us found pleasure, whenever possible, in focusing on one small task. One task, we often said, clears the mind. And each of us recognized that this small task of finding a bigger office meant we were succeeding. We were making a go of this thing called Blue Ribbon, which spoke to a deep desire, in each of us, to win. Or at least not lose.

Though neither of us was much of a talker, we brought out a chatty streak in each other. Those nights we discussed everything, opened up to each other with unusual candor. Woodell told me in detail about his injury. If I was ever tempted to take myself too seriously, Woodell's story always reminded me that things could be worse. And the way he handled himself was a constant, bracing lesson in the virtue, and value, of good spirits.

His injury wasn't typical, he said. And it wasn't total. He still had some feeling, still had hopes of marrying, having a family. He also had hopes of a cure. He was taking an experimental new drug, which had shown promise in paraplegics. Trouble was, it had a garlicky aroma. Some nights on our office-hunting expeditions Woodell would smell like an old-school pizzeria, and I'd let him hear about it.

I asked Woodell if he was—I hesitated, fearing I had no right—*happy*. He gave it some thought. Yes, he said. He was. He loved his work. He loved Blue Ribbon, though he sometimes cringed at the irony. A man who can't walk peddling shoes.

Not sure what to say to this, I said nothing.

Often Penny and I would have Woodell over to the new house for dinner. He was like family, we loved him, but we also knew we were filling a void in his life, a need for company and domestic comforts. So Penny always wanted to cook something special when Woodell came over, and the most special thing she could think of was Cornish game hen. Though hens put a serious dent in her twenty-five dollar grocery budget, Penny simply couldn't economize when it came to Woodell. If I told her that Woodell was coming to dinner, she'd reflexively gush: "I'll get some capons!" It was more than wanting to be hospitable. She was fattening him up. She was nurturing him. Woodell, I think, spoke to her newly activated maternal streak.

I struggle to remember. I close my eyes and think back, but so many precious moments from those nights are gone forever. Numberless conversations, breathless laughing fits. Declarations, revelations, confidences. They've all fallen into the sofa cushions of time. I remember only that we always sat up half the night, cataloging the past, mapping out the future. I remember that we took turns describing what our little company was, and what it might be, and what it must never be. How I wish, on just one of those nights, I'd had a tape recorder. Or kept a journal, as I did on my trip around the world.

Still, at least I can always call to mind the image of Woodell, seated at the head of our dinette, carefully dressed in his blue jeans, his trademark V-neck sweater over a white T. And always, on his feet, a pair of Tigers, the rubber soles pristine.

By then he'd grown a long beard, and a bushy mustache, both of which I envied. Heck, it was the sixties, I'd have had a beard down to my chin. But I was constantly needing to go to the bank and ask for money. I couldn't look like a bum when I presented myself to Wallace. A clean shave was one of my few concessions.

Woodell and I eventually found a promising office, in Tigard, south of downtown Portland. It wasn't a whole office building—we couldn't afford that—but a corner of one floor. The rest was occupied by the Horace Mann Insurance Company. Inviting, almost plush, it was a dramatic step up, and yet I hesitated. There had been a curious logic in our being next door to a honky-tonk. But an insurance company? With carpeted halls and watercoolers and men in tailored suits? The atmosphere was so button-down, so corporate. Our surroundings, I felt, had much to do with our spirit, and our spirit was a big part of our success, and I worried how our spirit might change if we were suddenly sharing space with a bunch of Organization Men and automatons.

I took to my recliner, gave it some thought, and decided a corporate vibe might be asymmetrical, contrary to our core beliefs, but it might also be just the thing with our bank. Maybe when Wallace saw our boring, sterile new office space, he'd treat us with respect. Also, the office was in Tigard. Selling Tigers out of Tigard—maybe it was meant to be.

Then I thought about Woodell. He said he was happy at Blue Ribbon, but he'd mentioned the irony. Maybe it was more than ironic, sending him out to high schools and colleges to sell Tigers out of his car. Maybe it was torture. And maybe it was a poor use of his talents. What suited Woodell best was bringing order to chaos, problem solving. One small task.

After he and I went together to sign the Tigard lease, I asked him if he'd like to change jobs, become operations manager for Blue Ribbon. No more sales calls. No more schools. Instead, he'd be in charge of dealing with all the things for which I didn't have the time and patience. Like talking to Bork in L.A. Or corresponding with Johnson in Wellesley. Or opening a new office in Miami. Or hiring someone to coordinate all the new sales reps and organize their reports. Or approving expense accounts. Best of all, Woodell would have to oversee the person who monitored company bank accounts. Now if he didn't cash his own paychecks, he'd have to explain the overage to his boss: himself.

Beaming, Woodell said he liked the sound of that very much. He reached out his hand. Deal, he said.

Still had the grip of an athlete.

Penny went to the doctor in September 1969. A checkup. The doctor said everything looked fine, but the baby was taking its time. Probably another week, he said.

The rest of that afternoon Penny spent at Blue Ribbon, helping customers. We went home together, ate an early dinner, turned in early. About 4:00 a.m. she jostled me. "I don't feel so good," she said. I phoned the doctor and told him to meet us at Emanuel Hospital.

In the weeks before Labor Day I'd made several practice trips to the hospital, and it was a good thing, because now, "game time," I was such a wreck that Portland looked to me like Bangkok. Everything was strange, unfamiliar. I drove slowly, to make sure of each turn. Not too slowly, I scolded myself, or you'll have to deliver the baby yourself. The streets were all empty, the lights were all green. A soft rain was falling. The only sounds in the car were Penny's heavy breaths and the wipers squeaking across the windshield. As I pulled up to the entrance of the emergency room, as I helped Penny into the hospital, she kept saying, "We're probably overreacting, I don't think it's time yet." Still, she was breathing the way I used to breathe in the final lap. I remember the nurse taking Penny from me, helping her into a wheelchair, rolling her down a hall. I followed along, trying to help. I had a pregnancy kit I'd packed myself, with a stopwatch, the same one I'd used to time

Woodell. I now timed Penny's contractions aloud. "Five . . . four . . . three . . ."

She stopped panting and turned to me. Through clenched teeth she said, "Stop . . . doing . . . that."

A nurse now helped her out of the wheelchair and onto a gurney and rolled her away. I stumbled back down the hall into something the hospital called "The Bullpen," where expectant fathers were expected to sit and stare into space. I would have been in the delivery room with Penny, but my father had warned me against it. He'd told me that I'd been born bright blue, which scared the daylights out of him, and he therefore cautioned me, "At the decisive moment, be somewhere else."

I sat in a hard plastic chair, eyes closed, doing shoe work in my mind. After an hour I opened my eyes and saw our doctor standing before me. Beads of sweat glistened on his forehead. He was saying something. That is, his lips were moving. But I couldn't hear. *Life's a joy? Here's a toy? Are you Roy?*

He said it again: It's a boy.

"A—a—boy? Really?"

"Your wife did a superb job," he was saying. "She did not complain once, and she pushed at all the right times—has she taken many Lamaze classes?"

"Lemans?" I said. "Pardon?"

"What?"

He led me like an invalid down a long hall and into a

small room. There, behind a curtain, was my wife, exhausted, radiant, her face bright red. Her arms were wrapped around a quilted white blanket decorated with blue baby carriages. I pushed back a corner of the blanket to reveal a head the size of a ripe grapefruit, a white stocking cap perched on top. My boy. He looked like a traveler. Which, of course, he was. He'd just begun his own trip around the world.

I leaned down, kissed Penny's cheek. I pushed away her damp hair. "You're a champion," I whispered. She squinted, uncertain. She thought I was talking to the baby.

She handed me my son. I cradled him in my arms. He was so alive, but so delicate, so helpless. The feeling was wondrous, different from all other feelings, though familiar, too. Please don't let me drop him.

At Blue Ribbon I spent so much time talking about quality control, about craftsmanship, about delivery—but this, I realized, this was the real thing. "We made this," I said to Penny. We. Made. This. She nodded, then lay back. I handed the baby to the nurse and told Penny to sleep. I floated out of the hospital and down to the car. I felt a sudden and overpowering need to see my father, a hunger for my father. I drove to his newspaper, parked several blocks away. I wanted to walk. The rain had stopped. The air was cool and damp. I ducked into a cigar store. I pictured myself handing my father a big fat robusto and saying, *Hiya, Grandpa!*

Coming out of the store, the wooden cigar box under my arm, I bumped straight into Keith Forman, a former runner at Oregon. "Keith!" I cried.

"Heya, Buck," he said.

I grabbed him by the lapels and shouted, "It's a boy!" He leaned away, confused. There wasn't time to explain. I kept walking.

Forman had been on the famous Oregon team that set the world record in the four-mile relay. As a runner, as an accountant, I always remembered their stunning time: 16:08.9. A star on Bowerman's 1962 national championship team, Forman had also been the fifth American ever to break the four-minute mile. And to think, I told myself, only hours ago I'd thought *those things* made a champion.

Fall. The woolen skies of November settled in low. I wore heavy sweaters, and sat by the fireplace, and did a sort of self-inventory. I was all stocked up on gratitude. Penny and my new son, whom we'd named Matthew, were healthy. Bork and Woodell and Johnson were happy. Sales continued to rise.

Then came the mail. A letter from Bork. After returning from Mexico City, he was suffering some sort of mental Montezuma's revenge. He had problems with me, he told me in the letter. He didn't like my management style, he didn't like my vision for the company, he didn't like what I was paying him.

He didn't understand why I took weeks to answer his letters, and sometimes didn't answer at all. He had ideas about shoe design, and he didn't like how they were being ignored. After several pages of all this he demanded immediate changes, plus a raise.

My second mutiny. This one, however, was more complicated than Johnson's. I spent several days drafting my reply. I agreed to raise his salary, slightly, and then I pulled rank. I reminded Bork that in any company there could only be one boss, and sadly for him the boss of Blue Ribbon was Buck Knight. I told him if he wasn't happy with me or my management style, he should know that quitting and being fired were both viable options.

As with my "spy memo," I suffered instant writer's remorse. The moment I dropped it in the mail I realized that Bork was a valuable part of the team, that I didn't want to lose him, that I couldn't afford to lose him. I dispatched our new operations manager, Woodell, to Los Angeles, to patch things up.

Woodell took Bork to lunch and tried to explain that I wasn't sleeping much, with a new baby and all. Also, Woodell told him, I was feeling tremendous stress after the visit from Kitami and Mr. Onitsuka. Woodell joked about my unique management style, telling Bork that everyone bitched about it, everyone pulled their hair out about my nonresponses to their memos and letters.

In all Woodell spent a few days with Bork, smoothing his feathers, going over the operation. He discovered that Bork was stressed, too. Though the retail store was thriving, the back room, which had basically become our national warehouse, was in shambles. Boxes everywhere, invoices and papers stacked to the ceiling. Bork couldn't keep pace.

When Woodell returned he gave me the picture. "I think Bork's back in the fold," he said, "but we need to relieve him of that warehouse. We need to transfer all warehouse operations up here." Moreover, he added, we needed to hire Woodell's mother to run it. She'd worked for years in the warehouse at Jantzen, the legendary Oregon outfitter, so it wasn't nepotism, he said. Ma Woodell was perfect for the job.

I wasn't sure I cared. If Woodell was good with it, I was good with it. Plus, the way I saw it: The more Woodells the better.

1970

I had to fly to Japan again, and this time two weeks before Christmas. I didn't like leaving Penny alone with Matthew, especially around the holidays, but it couldn't be avoided. I needed to sign a new deal with Onitsuka. Or not. Kitami was keeping me in suspense. He wouldn't tell me his thoughts about renewing me until I arrived.

Yet again I found myself at a conference table surrounded by Onitsuka executives. This time, Mr. Onitsuka didn't make his trademark late entrance, nor did he absent himself pointedly. He was there from the start, presiding.

He opened the meeting by saying that he intended to renew Blue Ribbon for another three years. I smiled for the first time in weeks. Then I pressed my advantage. I asked for a longer deal. Yes, 1973 seemed light-years away, but it would be here in a blink. I needed more time and security. My bankers needed more. "Five years?" I said.

Mr. Onitsuka smiled. "Three."

He then gave a strange speech. Notwithstanding several years of sluggish worldwide sales, he said, plus some strategic missteps, the outlook was rosy for Onitsuka. Through cost cutting and reorganization his company had regained its edge. Sales for the upcoming fiscal year were expected to top $22 million, a good portion of which would come from the United States. A recent survey showed that 70 percent of all American runners owned a pair of Tigers.

I knew that. Maybe I'd had a little something to do with that, I wanted to say. That's why I wanted a longer contract.

But Mr. Onitsuka said that one major reason for Onitsuka's solid numbers was . . . Kitami. He looked down the table, bestowed a fatherly smile on Kitami. Therefore, Mr. Onitsuka said, Kitami was being promoted. Henceforth he'd be the company's operations manager. He'd now be Onitsuka's Woodell, though I remember thinking that I wouldn't trade one Woodell for a thousand Kitamis.

With a bow of my head I congratulated Mr. Onitsuka on his company's good fortune. I turned and bowed my head at Kitami, congratulating him on his promotion. But when I raised my head and made eye contact with Kitami I saw in his gaze something cold. Something that stayed with me for days.

We drew up the agreement. It was four or five paragraphs, a flimsy thing. The thought crossed my mind that it should be more substantive, and that it would be nice to have a lawyer vet it. But there wasn't time. We all signed it, then moved on to other topics.

I was relieved to have a new contract, but I returned to Oregon feeling troubled, anxious, more so than at any time in the last eight years. Sure, my briefcase held a guarantee that Onitsuka would supply me with shoes for the next three years—but why were they refusing to extend beyond three? More to the point, the extension was misleading. Onitsuka was guaranteeing me a supply, but their supply was chronically, dangerously late. About which they still had a maddeningly blasé attitude. *Little more days.* With Wallace continually acting more like a loan shark than a banker, a little more days could mean disaster.

And when the shipments from Onitsuka did finally arrive? They often contained the wrong number of shoes. Often the wrong sizes. Sometimes the wrong models. This kind of disarray clogged our warehouse and rankled our sales reps. Before I left Japan Mr. Onitsuka and Kitami assured me that they were building new state-of-the-art factories. Delivery problems would soon be a thing of the past, they said. I was skeptical, but there was nothing I could do. I was at their mercy. Johnson, meanwhile, was losing his mind. His letters, once mumbly with angst, were becoming shrill with hysteria. The main problem was Bowerman's Cortez, he said. It was simply too popular. We'd gotten people hooked on the thing, turned them into full-blown Cortez addicts, and now we couldn't meet the demand, which created anger and resentment up and down the supply chain.

God, we are really screwing our customers, Johnson wrote. *Happiness is a boatload of Cortez; reality is a boatload of Bostons with steel wool uppers, tongues made out of old razor blades, sizes 6 to 6½.*

He was exaggerating, but not much. It happened all the time. I'd secure a loan from Wallace, then hang fire waiting for Onitsuka to send the shoes, and when the boat finally docked it wouldn't contain any Cortezes. Six weeks later, we'd get too many Cortezes, and by then it was too late.

Why? It couldn't just be Onitsuka's decrepit factories, we all agreed, and sure enough, Woodell eventually figured out that Onitsuka was satisfying its local customers in Japan *first,* then worrying about foreign exports. Terribly unfair, but again what could I do? I had no leverage.

Even if Onitsuka's new factories ended all delivery problems, even if every shipment of shoes hit the water right on time, with all the correct quantities of size 10s, and no size 5s, I'd still face problems with Wallace. Bigger orders would require bigger loans, and bigger loans would be harder to pay off, and in 1970 Wallace was telling me that he wasn't interested in playing that game anymore.

I recall one day, sitting in Wallace's office. Both he and White were working me over pretty good. Wallace seemed to be enjoying himself, though White kept giving me looks that said, *Sorry, pal, this is my job.* As always I politely took the abuse they dished out, playing the role of meek small business owner. Long on contrition, short on credit. I knew the role backward and forward, but I remember feeling that at any moment I might cut loose a bloodcurdling scream. Here I'd built this dynamic company, from nothing, and by all measures it was a beast—sales doubling every year, like clockwork—and this was the thanks I got? Two bankers treating me like a deadbeat?

White, trying to cool things off, said a few nominal things in support of Blue Ribbon. I watched his words have no effect whatsoever on Wallace. I took a breath, started to speak, then stopped. I didn't trust my voice. I just sat up straighter and hugged myself. This was my new nervous tic, my new habit. Rubber bands were no longer cutting it. Whenever I felt stressed, whenever I wanted to choke someone, I'd wrap my arms good and tight around my torso. That day the habit was more pronounced. I must have looked as if I were practicing some exotic yoga pose I'd learned in Thailand.

At issue was more than the old philosophical disagreement about growth. Blue Ribbon was approaching $600,000 in sales, and that day I'd gone in to ask for a loan of $1.2 million, a number that had symbolic meaning for Wallace. It was the first time I'd broken the million-dollar barrier. In his mind this was like the four-minute mile. Very few people were meant to break it. He was weary of this whole thing, he said, weary of me. For the umpteenth time he explained that he lived on cash balances, and for the umpteenth time I suggested ever so politely that if my sales and earnings were going up, up, up, Wallace should be happy to have my business.

Wallace rapped his pen on the table. My credit was maxed out, he said. Officially, irrevocably, immediately. He wasn't authorizing one more cent until I put some cash in my account and left it there. Meanwhile, henceforth, he'd be imposing strict sales quotas for me to meet. Miss one quota, he said, by even one day, and, well . . . He didn't finish the sentence. His voice trailed off, and I was left to fill the silence with worst-case scenarios.

I turned to White, who gave me a look. *What can I do, pal?*

Days later Woodell showed me a telex from Onitsuka. The big spring shipment was ready to hit the water and they wanted twenty thousand dollars. Great, we said. For once they're shipping the shoes on time.

Just one hitch. We didn't have twenty thousand dollars. And it was clear I couldn't go to Wallace. I couldn't ask Wallace for change of a five.

So I telexed Onitsuka and asked them to hold the shoes,

please, until we brought in some more revenue from our sales force. *Please don't think we are in financial difficulty*, I wrote. It wasn't a lie, per se. As I told Bowerman, we weren't broke, we just had no money. Lots of assets, no cash. We simply needed more time. Now it was my turn to say: *Little more days.*

While awaiting Onitsuka's response, I realized that there was only one way to solve this cash flow problem once and for all. A small public offering. If we could sell 30 percent of Blue Ribbon, at two bucks a share, we could raise $300,000 overnight.

The timing for such an offering seemed ideal. In 1970 the first-ever venture capital firms were starting to sprout up. The whole concept of venture capital was being invented before our eyes, though the idea of what constituted a sound investment for venture capitalists wasn't very broad. Most of the new venture capital firms were in Northern California, so they were mainly attracted to high-tech and electronics companies. Silicon Valley, almost exclusively. Since most of those companies had futuristic-sounding names, I formed a holding company for Blue Ribbon and gave it a name designed to attract tech-happy investors: Sports-Tek Inc.

Woodell and I sent out fliers advertising the offering, then sat back and braced for the clamorous response.

Silence.

A month passed.

Deafening silence.

No one phoned. Not one person.

That is, almost no one. We did manage to sell three hundred shares, at one dollar per.

To Woodell and his mother.

Ultimately we withdrew the offering. It was a humiliation, and in its wake I had many heated conversations with myself. I blamed the shaky economy. I blamed Vietnam. But first and foremost I blamed myself. I'd overvalued Blue Ribbon. I'd overvalued my life's work.

More than once, over my first cup of coffee in the morning, or while trying to fall asleep at night, I'd tell myself: Maybe I'm a fool? Maybe this whole damn shoe thing is a fool's errand?

Maybe, I thought.

Maybe.

I scraped together the twenty thousand dollars from our receivables, paid off the bank, and took delivery of the order from Onitsuka. Another sigh of relief. Followed by a tightening in the chest. What would I do the next time? And the next?

I needed cash. That summer was unusually warm. Languorous days of golden sunshine, clear blue skies, the world a paradise. It all seemed to mock me and my mood. If 1967 had been the Summer of Love, 1970 was the Summer of Liquidity, and I had none. I spent most of every day thinking about liquidity, talking about liquidity, looking to the heavens and pleading for liquidity. My kingdom for liquidity. An even more loathsome word than "equity."

Eventually I did what I didn't want to do, what I'd vowed never to do. I put the touch on anybody with ears. Friends, family, casual acquaintances. I even went with my hand out to former teammates, guys I'd sweated and trained and raced alongside. Including my former archrival, Grelle.

I'd heard that Grelle had inherited a pile from his grandmother. On top of that, he was involved in all sorts of lucrative business ventures. He worked as a salesman for two grocery store chains while selling caps and gowns to graduates on the side, and both ventures were said to be humming along. He also owned a great big chunk of land at Lake Arrowhead, someone said, and lived there in a rambling house. The man was born to win. (He was even still running competitively, one year away from becoming the best in the world.)

There was an all-comers road race in Portland that summer, and Penny and I invited a group of people to the house afterward, for a party. I made sure to invite Grelle, then waited for just the right moment. When everyone was rested, I asked Grelle for a word in private. I took him into my den and made my pitch short and sweet. New company, cash flow problems, considerable upside, yadda yadda. He was gracious, courteous, and smiled pleasantly. "I'm just not interested, Buck."

With nowhere else to turn, with no other options, I was sitting at my desk one day, staring out the window. Woodell knocked. He rolled into the office, closed the door. He said he and his parents wanted to loan me five thousand dollars, and they wouldn't take no for an answer. They also wouldn't tolerate any mention of interest. In fact, they wouldn't even formalize the loan with any sort of papers. He was going to Los Angeles to see Bork, but while he was gone, he said, I should drive to his house and collect the check from his folks.

Days later I did something beyond imagining, something I didn't think myself capable of doing. I drove to Woodell's house and asked for the check.

I knew the Woodells weren't well off. I knew that, with their son's medical bills, they were scuffling more than I. This five thousand dollars was their life savings. I knew that.

But I was wrong. His parents had a little bit more, and they asked if I needed that, too. And I said yes. And they gave me their last three thousand dollars, draining their savings down to zero.

How I wished I could put that check in my desk drawer and not cash it. But I couldn't. I wouldn't.

On my way out the door I stopped. I asked them: "Why are you doing this?"

"Because," Woodell's mother said, "if you can't trust the company your son is working for, then who can you trust?"

Penny was continuing to find creative ways of stretching her twenty-five-dollar grocery allowance, which meant fifty kinds of beef Stroganoff, which meant my weight ballooned. By the middle of 1970 I was around 190, an all-time high. One morning, getting dressed for work, I put on one of my baggier suits and it wasn't baggy. Standing before the mirror I said to my reflection: "Uh-oh."

But it was more than the Stroganoff. Somehow, I'd gotten out of the running habit. Blue Ribbon, marriage, fatherhood—there was never time. Also, I'd felt burned out. Though I'd loved running for Bowerman, I'd hated it, too. The same thing happens to all kinds of college athletes. Years of training and competing at a high level take their toll. You need a rest. But now the rest was over. I needed to get back out there. I didn't want to be the fat, flabby, sedentary head of a running-shoe company.

And if tight suits and the specter of hypocrisy weren't enough incentive, another motivation soon came along.

Shortly after that all-comers race, after Grelle refused me the loan, he and I went for a private run. Four miles in, I saw Grelle looking back at me sadly as I huffed and puffed to keep up. It was one thing to have him refuse me money, it was another to have him give me pity. He knew I was embarrassed, so he challenged me. "This fall," he said, "let's you and me race—one mile. I'll give you a full minute handicap, and if you beat me I'll pay you a buck for every second of difference in our times." I trained hard that summer. I got into the habit of running six miles every night after work. In no time I was back in shape, my weight down to 160. And when the day of the big race came—with Woodell on the stopwatch—I took thirty-six dollars from Grelle. (The victory was made all the sweeter the following week when Grelle jumped into an all-comers meet and ran 4:07.) As I drove home that day I felt immensely proud. Keep going, I told myself. Don't stop.

At almost the halfway mark of the year—June 15, 1970—I pulled my *Sports Illustrated* from my mailbox and got a shock. On the cover was a Man of Oregon. And not just any Man of Oregon, but perhaps the greatest of all time, greater even than Grelle. His name was Steve Prefontaine, and the photo showed him sprinting up the side of Olympus, aka Bowerman Mountain.

The article inside described Pre as an astonishing, once-a-generation phenom. He'd already made a big splash in high school, setting a national record (8:41) at two miles, but now, in his first year at Oregon, running two miles, he'd beaten Gerry Lindgren, who'd previously been considered unbeatable. And he'd beaten him by 27 seconds. Pre posted 8:40.0, third-fastest time in the nation that year. He'd also run three miles in 13:12.8, which in 1970 was faster than anyone, any-where, on earth.

Bowerman told the writer from *Sports Illustrated* that Pre was the fastest middle-distance runner alive. I'd never heard such unbridled enthusiasm from my stolid coach. In the days ahead, in other articles I clipped, Bowerman was even more effusive, calling Pre "the best runner I've ever had." Bowerman's assistant, Bill Dellinger, said Pre's secret weapon was his con-fidence, which was as freakish as his lung capacity. "Usually," Dellinger said, "it takes our guys twelve years to build confi-dence in themselves, and here's a young man who has the right attitude naturally."

Yes, I thought. Confidence. More than equity, more than liquidity, that's what a man needs.

I wished I had more. I wished I could borrow some. But confidence was cash. You had to have some to get some. And people were loath to give it to you.

Another revelation came that summer via another mag-azine. Flipping through *Fortune* I spotted a story about my former boss in Hawaii. In the years since I'd worked for Ber-nie Cornfeld and his Investors Overseas Services, he'd become even richer. He'd abandoned Dreyfus Funds and begun sell-ing shares in his own mutual funds, along with gold mines, real estate, and sundry other things. He'd built an empire, and as all empires eventually do it was now crumbling. I was so startled by news of his downfall that I dazedly turned the page and happened on another article, a fairly dry analysis of Japan's newfound economic power. Twenty-five years after Hiroshima, the article said, Japan was reborn. The world's third-largest economy, it was taking aggressive steps to become even larger, to consolidate its position and extend its reach. Besides simply outthinking and outworking other countries, Japan was adopting ruthless trade policies. The article then sketched the main vehicle for these trade policies, Japan's hyperaggressive *sogo shosha*. Trading companies.

It's hard to say exactly what those first Japanese trading companies were. Sometimes they were importers, scouring the globe and acquiring raw materials for companies that didn't have the means to do so. Other times they were exporters, representing those same companies overseas. Sometimes they were private banks, providing all kinds of companies with easy terms of credit. Other times they were an arm of the Japanese government.

I filed away all this information. For a few days. And the next time I went down to First National, the next time Wallace made me feel like a bum, I walked out and saw the sign for Bank of Tokyo. I'd seen that sign a hundred times before, of course, but now it meant something different. Huge pieces of the puzzle fell into place. Dizzy, I walked directly across the street, straight into the Bank of Tokyo, and presented myself to the woman at the front desk. I said I owned a shoe company, which was importing shoes from Japan, and I wanted to speak with someone about doing a deal. The woman instantly and discreetly led me to a back room. And left me.

After two minutes a man walked in and sat down very quietly at the table. He waited. I waited. He continued waiting. Finally I spoke.

"I have a company," I said.

"Yes?" he said.

"A shoe company," I said.

"Yes?" he said. I opened my briefcase. "These are my financial statements. I'm in a terrible bind. I need credit. I just read an article in *Fortune* about Japanese trading companies, and the article said these companies are looser with credit—and, well, do you know of any such companies that you might introduce me to?"

The man smiled. He'd read the same article. He said it just so happened that Japan's sixth-largest trading company had an office right above our heads, on the top floor of that building. All the major Japanese trading companies had offices in Portland, he said, but this particular one, Nissho Iwai, was the only one in Portland with its own commodities department. "It's a one hundred billion dollar company," the banker said, eyes widening.

"Oh, boy," I said.

"Please wait," he said. He left the room.

Minutes later he returned with an executive from Nissho Iwai. His name was Cam Murakami. We shook hands and chatted, strictly hypothetically, about the possibility of Nissho financing my future imports. I was intrigued. He was quite intrigued. He offered me a deal on the spot, and extended his hand, but I couldn't shake it. Not yet. First, I had to clear it with Onitsuka.

I sent a wire that day to Kitami, asking if he'd have any objections to my doing side business with Nissho. Days passed. Weeks. With Onitsuka, silence meant something. No news was bad news, no news was good news—but no news was always some sort of news.

While waiting to hear back, I got a troubling call. A shoe distributor on the East Coast said he'd been approached by Onitsuka about becoming its new U.S. distributor. I made him say it again, slower. He did. He said he wasn't trying to make me angry. Nor was he trying to help me out or give me a heads-up. He just wanted to know the status of my deal.

I began to shake. My heart was pounding. Months after signing a new contract with me, Onitsuka was plotting to break it? Had they been spooked when I was late taking delivery of the spring shipment? Had Kitami simply decided he didn't care for me?

My only hope was that this distributor on the East Coast was lying. Or mistaken. Maybe he'd misunderstood Onitsuka. Maybe it was a language thing?

I wrote to Fujimoto. I said I hoped he was still enjoying the bicycle I bought him. (Subtle.) I asked him to find out anything he could.

He wrote back right away. The distributor was telling the truth. Onitsuka was considering a clean break with Blue Ribbon, and Kitami was in touch with several distributors in the United States. There was no firm plan to break my contract, Fujimoto added, but candidates were being vetted and scouted.

I tried to focus on the good. There was no firm plan. This meant there was still hope. I could still restore Onitsuka's faith, change Kitami's mind. I would just need to remind Kitami of what Blue Ribbon was, and who I was. Which would mean inviting him to the United States for a friendly visit.

1971

Guess who's coming to dinner," Woodell said.

He wheeled into my office and handed me the telex. Kitami had accepted my invitation. He was coming to Portland to spend a few days. Then he was going to make a wider tour of the United States, for reasons he declined to share. "Visiting other potential distributors," I said to Woodell. He nodded.

It was March 1971. We vowed that Kitami was going to have the time of his life, that he would return home feeling love in his heart for America, Oregon, Blue Ribbon—and me. When we were done with him he'd be incapable of doing business with anyone else. And so, we agreed, the visit should close on a high note, with a gala dinner at the home of our prize asset—Bowerman.

In mounting this charm offensive, naturally I enlisted Penny. Together we met Kitami's flight, and together we whisked him straight to the Oregon coast, to her parents' oceanfront cottage.

Kitami had a companion with him, a sort of bag carrier, personal assistant, amanuensis, named Hiraku Iwano. He was just a kid, naïve, innocent, in his early twenties, and Penny had him eating out of her hand before we hit Sunset Highway.

We both slaved to give the two men an idyllic Pacific Northwest weekend. We sat on the porch with them and breathed in the sea air. We took them for long walks on the beach. We tried to focus most of our attention on Kitami, but both Penny and I found it easier to talk to Iwano, who read books and seemed guileless. Kitami seemed like a man who was importing guile by the boatload. Monday, bright and early, I drove Kitami back to Portland, to First National Bank. Just as I was determined to charm him on this trip, I thought that he could be helpful in charming Wallace, that he could vouch for Blue Ribbon and make credit easier to get.

White met us in the lobby and walked us into a conference room. I looked around. "Where's Wallace?" I asked.

"Ah," White said, "he won't be able to join us today."

What? That was the whole point of visiting the bank. I wanted Wallace to hear Kitami's ringing endorsement. Oh well, I thought— good cop will just have to relay the endorsement to bad cop.

I said a few preliminary words, expressed confidence that Kitami could bolster First National's faith in Blue Ribbon, then turned the floor over to Kitami, who scowled and did the one thing guaranteed to make my life harder. "Why do you not give my friends more *money?*" he said to White.

"W-w-what?" White said.

"Why do you refuse to extend credit to Blue Ribbon?" Kitami said, pounding his fist on the table.

"Well now—" White said.

Kitami cut him off. "What kind of bank is this? I do not understand! Maybe Blue Ribbon would be better off without you!"

White turned white. I tried to jump in. I tried to rephrase what Kitami was saying, tried to blame the language barrier, but the meeting was over. White stormed out, and I stared in astonishment at Kitami, who was wearing an expression that said, *Job well done.*

I drove Kitami to our new offices in Tigard and showed him around, introduced him to the gang. I was fighting hard to maintain my composure, to remain pleasant, to block out all thoughts about what had just happened. I was afraid that at any second I might lose it. But when I settled Kitami into a chair across from my desk, it was he who lost it—at me. "Blue Ribbon sales are disappointing!" he said. "You should be doing much better."

Stunned, I said that our sales were doubling every year.

Not good enough, he snapped. "Should be triple some people say," he said.

"What people?" I asked.

"Never mind," he said.

He took a folder from his briefcase, flipped it open, read it, snapped it shut. He repeated that he didn't like our numbers, that he didn't think we were doing enough. He opened the folder again, shut it again, shoved it back into his briefcase. I tried to defend myself, but he waved his hand in disgust. Back and forth we went, for quite a while, civil but tense.

After nearly an hour of this he stood and asked to use the men's room. Down the hall, I said.

The moment he was out of sight I jumped from behind my desk. I opened his briefcase and rummaged through and took out what looked like the folder he'd been referring to. I slid it under my desk blotter, then jumped behind my desk and put my elbows on the blotter. Waiting for Kitami to return, I had the strangest thought. I recalled all the times I'd volunteered with the Boy Scouts, all the times I'd sat on Eagle Scout review boards, handing out merit badges for honor and integrity. Two or three weekends a year I'd question pink-cheeked boys about their probity, their honesty, and now I was stealing documents from another man's briefcase? I was headed down a dark path. No telling where it might lead. Wherever, there was no getting around one immediate consequence of my actions. I'd have to recuse myself from the next review board.

How I longed to study the contents of that folder, and photocopy every scrap of paper in it, and go over it all with Woodell. But Kitami was soon back. I let him resume scolding me about sluggish numbers, let him talk himself out, and when he stopped I summed up my position. Calmly I said that Blue Ribbon might increase its sales if we could order more shoes, and we might order more shoes if we had more financing, and our bank might give us more financing if we had more security, meaning a longer contract with Onitsuka. Again he waved his hand. "Excuses," he said.

I raised the idea of funding our orders through a Japanese trading company, like Nissho Iwai, as I'd mentioned in my wire months before. "Bah," he said, "trading companies. They send money first—men later. Take over! Work way into your company, then take over." Translation: Onitsuka was only manufacturing a quarter of its own shoes, subcontracting the other three-quarters. Kitami was afraid that Nissho would find Onitsuka's network of factories, then go right around Onitsuka and become a manufacturer and put Onitsuka out of business.

Kitami stood. He needed to go back to his hotel, he said, have a rest. I said I'd have someone drive him, and I'd meet him for a cocktail later at his hotel bar.

The instant he was gone I went and found Woodell and told him what had happened. I held up the folder. "I stole *this* from his briefcase," I said.

"You did *what?*" Woodell said. He started to act appalled, but he was just as curious as I was about the folder's contents.

Together we opened it and laid it on his desk and found that it contained, among other things, a list of eighteen athletic shoe distributors across the United States and a schedule of appointments with half of them.

So there it was. In black and white. Some people say. The "some people" damning Blue Ribbon, poisoning Kitami against us, were our competitors. And he was on his way to visit them. Kill one East Coast Cowboy, twenty more rise up to take his place.

I was outraged, of course. But mostly hurt. For seven years we'd devoted ourselves to Tiger shoes. We'd introduced them to America, we'd reinvented the line. Bowerman and Johnson had shown Onitsuka how to make a better shoe, and their designs were now foundational, setting sales records, changing the face of the industry—and this was how we were repaid? "And now," I said to Woodell, "I have to go meet this Judas."

First I went for a six-mile run. I don't know when I've run harder, or been less present in my body. With each stride I yelled at the trees, screamed at the cobwebs hanging in the branches. It helped. By the time I'd showered and dressed and driven to

215

meet Kitami at his hotel, I was almost serene. Or maybe I was in shock. What Kitami said during that hour together, what I said—no memory. The next thing I remember is this. The following morning, when Kitami came to the office, Woodell and I ran a sort of shell game. While someone whisked Kitami into the coffee room, Woodell blocked the door to my office with his wheelchair and I slid the folder back into the briefcase.

On the last day of Kitami's visit, hours before the big dinner party, I hurried down to Eugene to confer with Bowerman and his lawyer, Jaqua. I left Penny to drive Kitami down later in the day, thinking: What's the worst that could happen?

Cut to Penny, hair disheveled, dress smeared with grease, pulling up to Bowerman's house. She took me aside and explained that they'd had a flat. "That creep," she whispered, "*stayed in the car—on the highway—and let me fix the tire all by myself!*" I steered her inside. Mrs. Bowerman gathered us all in the living room. "Welcome to our distinguished guests," she announced.

Applause.

For Kitami, this trip to the United States—the visit to the bank, the meetings with me, the dinner with the Bowermans—wasn't about Blue Ribbon. Nor was it about Onitsuka. Like everything else, it was all about Kitami.

• • •

Kitami left Portland the next day on his not-so-secret mission, his Give-Blue-Ribbon-the-Brush-Off tour of America. I asked again about his destination, and again he didn't answer. *Yoi tabi de arimas yoh ni*, I said. Safe travels.

I'd recently commissioned Hayes, my old boss from Price Waterhouse, to do some consulting work for Blue Ribbon, and now I huddled with him and tried to decide my next move before Kitami's return. We agreed that the best thing to do was keep the peace, try to convince Kitami not to leave us, not to abandon us. As angry and wounded as I was, I needed to accept that Blue Ribbon would be lost without Onitsuka. I needed, Hayes said, to stick with the devil I knew, and persuade him to stick with the devil *he* knew.

Later that week, when the devil returned, I invited him out to Tigard for one more visit before his flight home. Again I tried to rise above it all. I brought him into the conference room, and with Woodell and I on one side of the table, and Kitami and his assistant, Iwano, on the other, I screwed a big smile onto my face and said that we hoped he'd enjoyed his visit to our country.

He said yet again that he was disappointed in the performance of Blue Ribbon.

This time, however, he said he had a solution. "Shoot," I said.

"Sell us your company."

He said it so very softly. The thought crossed my mind that

some of the hardest things ever said in our lifetimes are said softly.

"Excuse me?" I said.

"Onitsuka Company Limited will buy controlling interest in Blue Ribbon, fifty-one percent. It is best deal for your company. And you. You would be wise to accept."

A takeover. *A hostile freaking takeover.* I looked at the ceiling. *You gotta be kidding,* I thought. Of all the arrogant, underhanded, ungrateful, bullying—

"And if we do not?"

"We will have no choice but to set up superior distributors."

"Superior. Uh-huh. I see. And what about our written agreement?"

He shrugged. So much for agreements.

I couldn't let my mind go to any of those places it was trying to go. I couldn't tell Kitami what I thought of him, or where to stick his offer, because Hayes was right, I *still* needed him. I had no backup, no plan B, no exit strategy. If I was going to save Blue Ribbon, I needed to do it slowly, on my own schedule, so as not to spook customers and retailers. I needed time, and therefore I needed Onitsuka to keep sending me shoes for as long as possible.

"Well," I said, fighting to control my voice, "I have a partner, of course. Coach Bowerman. I'll have to discuss your offer with him."

I was certain Kitami would see through this amateurish

stall. But he rose, hitched his pants, and smiled. "Talk it over with Dr. Bowerman. Get back to me."

I wanted to hit him. Instead, I shook his hand. He and Iwano walked out.

In the suddenly Kitami-less conference room, Woodell and I stared into the grain of the conference table and let the stillness settle over us.

I sent my budget and forecast for the coming year to First National, with my standard credit request. I wanted to send a note of apology, begging forgiveness for the Kitami debacle, but I knew White would roll with it. And besides, Wallace hadn't been there. Days after White got my budget and forecast he told me to come on down, he was ready to talk things over.

I wasn't in the hard little chair across from his desk more than two seconds before he delivered the news. "Phil, I'm afraid First National will not be able to do business any longer with Blue Ribbon. We will issue no more letters of credit on your behalf. We will pay off your last remaining shipments as they come in with what remains in your account—but when that last bill is paid, our relationship will be terminated."

I could see by White's waxy pallor that he was stricken. He'd had no part in this. This was coming from on high. Thus, there was no point in arguing. I spread my arms. "What do I do, Harry?"

"Find another bank."

"And if I can't? I'm out of business, right?"

He looked down at his papers, stacked them, fastened them with a paper clip. He told me that the question of Blue Ribbon had deeply divided the bank officers. Some were for us, some were against. Ultimately it was Wallace who'd cast the deciding vote. "I'm sick about this," White said. "So sick that I'm taking a sick day."

I didn't have that option. I staggered out of First National and drove straight to U.S. Bank. I pleaded with them to take me in.

Sorry, they said.

They had no desire to buy First National's secondhand problems.

Three weeks passed. The company, my company, born from nothing, and now finishing 1971 with sales of $1.3 million, was on life support. I talked with Hayes. I talked with my father. I talked with every other accountant I knew, one of whom mentioned that Bank of California had a charter allowing it to do business in three western states, including Oregon. Plus, Bank of Cal had a branch in Portland. I hurried over and, indeed, they welcomed me, gave me shelter from the storm. And a small line of credit.

Still, it was only a short-term solution. They were a bank, after all, and banks were, by definition, risk-averse. Regardless of my sales, Bank of California would soon view my zero cash balances with alarm. I needed to start preparing for that rainy day.

My thoughts kept returning to that Japanese trading company. Nissho. Late at night I'd think, They have $100 billion in sales . . . and they want desperately to help *me*. Why?

For starters, Nissho did huge volumes on low net margins, and therefore it loved growth companies with big upsides. That was us. In spades. In the eyes of Wallace and First National we'd been a land mine; to Nissho we were a potential gold mine.

So I went back. I met with the man sent from Japan to run the new general commodities department, Tom Sumeragi. A graduate of Tokyo University, the Harvard of Japan, Sumeragi looked strikingly like the great film actor Toshiro Mifune, who was famous for his portrayal of Miyamoto Musashi, the epic samurai duelist and author of a timeless manual on combat and inner strength, *The Book of Five Rings*.

He told me that Nissho was willing to take a second position to the bank on their loans. That would certainly quell my bankers. He also offered this nugget of information: Nissho had recently dispatched a delegation to Kobe, to investigate financing shoes for us, and to convince Onitsuka to let such a deal go through. But Onitsuka had thrown the Nissho delegation out. A $25 million company throwing out a $100 billion company? Nissho was embarrassed, and angry. "We can introduce you to many quality sports shoe manufacturers in Japan," Sumeragi said, smiling.

I pondered. I still held out some hope that Onitsuka would come to its senses. And I worried about a paragraph in our written agreement that forbade me from importing other brands of track-and-field shoes. "Maybe down the road," I said.

Sumeragi nodded. All in good time.

Reeling from all this drama, I was deeply tired when I returned home each night. But I'd always get a second wind after my six-mile run, followed by a hot shower and a quick dinner, alone. (Penny and Matthew ate around four.) I'd always try to find time to tell Matthew a bedtime story, and I'd always try to find a bedtime story that would be educational. I invented a character called Matt History, who looked and acted a lot like Matthew Knight, and I inserted him into the center of every yarn. Matt History was there at Valley Forge with George Washington. Matt History was there in Massachusetts with John Adams. Matt History was there when Paul Revere rode through the dark of night on a borrowed horse, warning John Hancock that the British were coming. "Hard on Revere's heels was a precocious young horseman from the suburbs of Portland, Oregon . . ."

Matthew would always laugh, delighted to find himself

caught up in these adventures. He'd sit up straighter in bed. He'd beg for more, more.

When Matthew was asleep, Penny and I would talk about the day. She'd often ask what we were going to do if it all went south. I'd say, "I can always fall back on accounting." I did not sound sincere, because I wasn't. I was not delighted to be caught up in these adventures.

Eventually Penny would look away, watch TV, resume her needlepoint, or read, and I'd retreat to my recliner, where I'd administer the nightly self-catechism.

What do you know?

I know Onitsuka can't be trusted.

What else do you know?

I know my relationship with Kitami can't be salvaged.

What does the future hold?

One way or another, Blue Ribbon and Onitsuka are going to break up. I just need to stay together as long as possible while I develop other supply sources, so I can manage the breakup.

What's Step One?

I need to scare off all the other distributors Onitsuka has lined up to replace me. Blast them right out of the water, by firing off letters threatening to sue if they breach my contract.

What's Step Two?

Find my own replacement for Onitsuka.

I flashed on a factory I'd heard about, in Guadalajara, the

223

one where Adidas had manufactured shoes during the 1968 Olympics, allegedly to skirt Mexican tariffs. The shoes were good, as I recalled. So I set up a meeting with the factory managers.

Even though it was in central Mexico, the factory was called Canada. Right away I asked the managers why. They chose the name, they said, because it sounded foreign, exotic. I laughed. Canada? Exotic? It was more comic than exotic, not to mention confusing. A factory south of the border named for a country north of the border.

Oh well. I didn't care. After looking the place over, after taking inventory of their present line of shoes, after surveying their leather room, I was impressed. The factory was big, clean, well run. Plus, it was Adidas-endorsed. I told them I'd like to place an order. Three thousand pairs of leather soccer shoes, which I planned to sell as football shoes. The factory owners asked me about the name of my brand. I told them I'd have to get back to them on that.

They handed me the contract. I looked at the dotted line above my name. Pen in hand, I paused. The question was now officially on the table. Was this a violation of my deal with Onitsuka?

Technically, no. My deal said I could import only Onitsuka track and field shoes, no others; it said nothing about importing someone else's *football* shoes. So I knew this contract with Canada wouldn't violate the letter of my Onitsuka deal. But the spirit?

Six months previously I would never have done this. Things were different now. Onitsuka had already broken the spirit of our deal, and my spirit, so I pulled the cap off my pen and signed the contract. I signed the heck out of that Canada contract. Then I went out for Mexican food.

Now about that logo. My new soccer-qua-football shoe would need something to set it apart from the stripes of Adidas and Onitsuka. I recalled that young artist I'd met at Portland State. What was her name? Oh, yes, Carolyn Davidson. She'd been in the office a number of times, doing brochures and ad slicks. When I got back to Oregon I invited her to the office again and told her we needed a logo.

"What kind?" she asked.

"I don't know," I said.

"That gives me a lot to go on," she said.

"Something that evokes a sense of motion," I said.

"Motion," she said, dubious.

She looked confused. Of course she did, I was babbling. I wasn't sure exactly what I wanted. I wasn't an artist. I showed her the soccer-football shoe and said, unhelpfully: "This. We need something for this."

She said she'd give it a try.

"Motion," she mumbled, leaving my office. Motion.

Two weeks later she came back with a portfolio of rough sketches. They were all variations on a single theme, and the theme seemed to be . . . fat lightning bolts? Chubby check marks? Morbidly obese squiggles? Her designs did evoke motion, of a kind, but also motion sickness. None spoke to me. I singled out a few that held out some promise and asked her to work with those.

Days later—or was it weeks?—Carolyn returned and spread a second series of sketches across the conference table. She also hung a few on the wall. She'd done several dozen more variations on the original theme, but with a freer hand. These were better. Closer.

Woodell and I and a few others looked them over. I remember Johnson being there, too, though why he'd come out from Wellesley, I can't recall. Gradually we inched toward a consensus. We liked . . . *this one* . . . slightly more than the others.

It looks like a wing, one of us said.

It looks like a whoosh of air, another said.

It looks like something a runner might leave in his or her wake. We all agreed it looked new, fresh, and yet somehow— ancient.

Timeless.

For her many hours of work, we gave Carolyn our deepest thanks and a check for thirty-five dollars, then sent her on her way.

After she left we continued to sit and stare at this one logo, which we'd sort of selected, and sort of settled on by default. "Something eye-catching about it," Johnson said. Woodell agreed.

I frowned, scratched my cheek. "You guys like it more than I do," I said. "But we're out of time. It'll have to do."

"You don't like it?" Woodell said.

I sighed. "I don't love it. Maybe it will grow on me." We sent it to Canada.

Now we just needed a name to go with this logo I didn't love.

Over the next few days we kicked around dozens of ideas, until two leading candidates emerged.

Falcon.

And Dimension Six.

I was partial to the latter, because I was the one who came up with it. Woodell and everyone else told me that it was god-awful. It wasn't catchy, they said, and it didn't mean anything.

We took a poll of all our employees. Secretaries, accountants, sales reps, retail clerks, file clerks, warehouse workers—we demanded that each person jump in, make at least one suggestion. Ford had just paid a top-flight consulting firm $2 million to come up with the name of its new Maverick, I announced to everyone. "We haven't got two million dollars—but we've got fifty smart people, and we can't do any worse than ... *Maverick*."

Also, unlike Ford, we had a deadline. Canada was starting production on the shoe that Friday.

Hour after hour was spent arguing and yelling, debating the virtue of this name or that. Someone liked Bork's suggestion, Bengal. Someone else said the only possible name was Condor. I huffed and groused. "Animal names," I said. "*Animal* names! We've considered the name of just about every animal in the forest. *Must* it be an animal?"

Again and again I lobbied for Dimension Six. Again and again I was told by my employees that it was unspeakably bad.

Someone, I forget who, summed up the situation neatly. "All these names ... suck." I thought it might have been Johnson, but all the documentation says he'd left and gone back to Wellesley by then.

One night, late, we were all tired, running out of patience. If I heard one more animal name I was going to jump out a window. Tomorrow's another day, we said, drifting out of the office, headed out to our cars.

I went home and sat in my recliner. My mind went back and forth, back and forth. Falcon? Bengal? Dimension Six? Something else? Anything else?

The day of decision arrived. Canada had already started producing the shoes, and samples were ready to go in Japan, but before anything could be shipped, we needed to choose a name. Also, we had magazine ads slated to run, to coincide with the shipments, and we needed to tell the graphic artists what name to put in the ads. Finally, we needed to file paperwork with the U.S. Patent Office.

Woodell wheeled into my office. "Time's up," he said.

I rubbed my eyes. "I know."

"What's it going to be?"

"I don't know."

My head was splitting. By now the names had all run together into one mind-melting glob. *Falconbengaldimensionsix.*

"There is . . . one more suggestion," Woodell said.

"From who?"

"Johnson phoned first thing this morning," he said. "Apparently a new name came to him in a dream last night."

I rolled my eyes. "A dream?"

"He's serious," Woodell said.

"He's always serious."

"He says he sat bolt upright in bed in the middle of the night and saw the name before him," Woodell said.

"What is it?" I asked, bracing myself.

"Nike."

"Huh?"

"Nike."

"Spell it."

"N-I-K-E," Woodell said.

I wrote it on a yellow legal pad.

The Greek goddess of victory. The Acropolis. The Parthenon. The Temple. I thought back. Briefly. Fleetingly.

"We're out of time," I said. "Nike. Falcon. Or Dimension Six."

"Everyone hates Dimension Six."

"Everyone but me."

He frowned. "It's your call."

He left me. I made doodles on my pad. I made lists, crossed them out. Tick, tock, tick, tock.

I needed to telex the factory—now.

I hated making decisions in a hurry, and that's all I seemed to do in those days. I looked to the ceiling. I gave myself two more minutes to mull over the different options, then walked down the hall to the telex machine. I sat before it, gave myself three more minutes.

Reluctantly, I punched out the message. *Name of new brand is . . .*

A lot of things were rolling around in my head, consciously, unconsciously. First, Johnson had pointed out that seemingly all iconic brands—Clorox, Kleenex, Xerox—have short names. Two syllables or less. And they always have a strong sound in the name, a letter like "K" or "X," that sticks in the mind. That all made sense. And that all described Nike.

Also, I liked that Nike was the goddess of victory. What's more important, I thought, than victory?

I might have heard, in the far recesses of my mind, Churchill's voice. *You ask, What is our aim? I can answer in one word. It is victory.* I might have recalled the victory medal awarded to all veterans of World War II, a bronze medallion with Athena Nike on the front, breaking a sword in two. I might have. Sometimes I believe that I did. But in the end I don't really know what led me to my decision. Luck? Instinct? Some inner spirit?

Yes.

"What'd you decide?" Woodell asked me at the end of the day.

"Nike," I mumbled.

"Hm," he said.

"Yeah, I know," I said.

"Maybe it'll grow on us," he said.

Maybe.

1972–1980
The Highlights

The name Nike did grow on me—at least by fits and starts—kind of like the business itself.

And in the years that followed the picking of our name, the business operated at two extremes: terrific and on the edge of disaster. Often those two extremes existed at the same time.

The Nike brand made its national debut at the Sporting Goods Show in Chicago in February 1972. We had appeared there several times as the national distributor for Tiger shoes, but this was different. Totally different. This was everything. Our new line would get at least a minimum level of acceptance, or . . . or we would all be looking for work.

When the samples from the first production run arrived, we were even more on edge. The originals had been works of art. These were not. Glue slopped over the midsoles and the stitch lines were crooked. The shoes would function but they didn't look as good as their originals. And the most popular models of the Tiger were there with our trademark stripe. After all, we had designed and named them for Tiger.

We were very much on edge when the doors opened. But we felt so much better when they closed. The retailers came to look, and then they ordered. More than we expected, and more than what we needed. We were alive.

Two weeks later, Kitami was on his way to Oregon. We met in Eugene, and Kitami expressed deep regret at our "betrayal," then handed a notice of termination. Jaqua suggested we discuss this. Kitami was adamant, but did propose that Bill Bowerman become a paid consultant of Onitsuka Co. Ltd. Bowerman was so shocked, he was momentarily speechless, then conveyed in quite clear language that that was never going to happen. The room was filled with tension as the meeting broke.

So that was it.

We were on our own. With an unproven source of supply and a brand no one had heard of.

After a long week, we had Johnson fly out for an all-hands meeting in Beaverton.

I gave it my all, explaining why, in the long run, we were fortunate that this had happened.

"This is our moment. No more selling someone else's brand. Nor more working for someone else. Onituska's late deliveries, mixed-up orders, refusal to hear and implement our design ideas—they are no more. If we're going to succeed, or fail, we should do so on our own terms, with our own ideas—our own brand. The two millions sales we posted last year were way more a product of our ingenuity and hard work, than of Onitsuka's. This is our liberation. Our Independence Day."

It wasn't as if anybody really believed we were lucky this happened. But what they did feel, unanimously, was relief. We had a chance. We were still alive.

The biggest track meet every four years is the Olympic Games. The second biggest is the U.S. Olympic Trials. That June the trials were held for the first time ever in Eugene.

We set up operations in Geoff Hollister's Eugene store, passing out free shoes to top competitors who were interested enough to take them. Penny silk-screened T-shirts in the back room with the athletes' names on them.

We gave out a free pair of shoes to the great USC long jumper Jesse Williams, then an hour later a man claiming to be Jesse Williams came in for a free pair. To this day I don't know which was the real Jesse Williams, but we didn't take a chance. We gave the second Jesse a free pair of shoes.

The spikes were not good enough yet. Not a single finalist was in our spikes, but lots of training shoes were worn, and about 25 percent of the marathoners were in one model or another of the new Nike racing flats. And while we did not qualify anyone for the team, we did finish fourth, fifth, sixth, and seventh. Considering the short time we had to work we were pretty happy with that.

But the final was what we were all waiting for—the last event of the trials—the 5,000 between Oregon's twenty-two-year-old Steve Prefontaine (known as Pre) vs. three-time Olympian, thirty-four-year-old George Young. It was more like a bullfight than a distance race.

Pre broke first with the gun, Young right next. At the one mile they were ten yards clear of the field. Young stayed within a stride of Pre for the next seven laps, and on each one of those laps the decibel level at Hayward Field rose.

And then in the last lap, Pre opened up one yard. Then two, then three, and finally ten before the tape. The last lap was deafening and both runners broke the American record.

As we filed out of the stadium that day, we resolved to be like Pre: resilient, courageous. We would fight. He would be our exemplar, our North Star.

1972

We looked forward to the Munich Olympics with excitement. Bowerman was head coach of the track team and Pre had (as always) made brash predictions even though Lasse Viren of Finland was the overwhelming favorite and defending champion. Pre announce he was ready to run the last mile in the 3 ⅛ mile race in under four minutes.

But before the competition had begun, Bowerman had managed to irritate the entire Munich Organizing Committee by announcing things were not well organized and, in particular, security was unsatisfactory.

Controversies seemed to happen every day. A change in the start time for 100-meter heats was announced in a printout buried within hundreds of pages of other material. Two of the three American sprinters did not even start their races.

World pole vault record holder Bob Seagren had his pole declared illegal. Vaulting with a strange implement, he did not medal.

Pre made the final. He went into the last lap of the final right on the heels of Viren and Mohammed Gammoudi, challenged them on the back stretch, took the lead for a few strides, but then was held off on the curve. Viren and Gammoudi pulled away in the home stretch and the dying Pre was caught by Ian Stewart of England, who edged him out for third and the bronze medal.

Pre was devastated. When told everyone in Eugene was proud of him and should name a street after him, he asked, "Yeah, what are they going to name it . . . fourth?"

But Pre's defeat was overshadowed by the big tragedy. Eight masked gunmen stole into the Olympic compound and kidnapped eleven Israeli athletes. They were bussed to the Munich airport and assassinated on the tarmac.

On conclusion of the games I drove to Eugene to see Bowerman. I had never seen him so deflated. The Olympics were the pinnacle of achievement for any track person. *His* Olympics had been a disaster.

A month later, Bowerman retired as the University track and field coach.

There was lots going on on the business side as well. We had Jeff Johnson and Bob Woodell switch positions. Sounds simple, but they completely uplifted their lives to make it happen—all for the good of the cause. Jeff moved from his beloved New England to Beaverton where he could use his budding design talents better and Bob moved to Exeter, New Hampshire, where his administrative talents could oversee our sales and warehousing.

Onitsuka sued us in Japan for breach of contract, which left us no choice but to counter in the U.S. Question: How to have a lawsuit with no money? Answer: Get Cousin Houser to take the case on a contingent fee basis. Cousin Houser may have agreed to that in a moment of weakness. We were slow paying the travel expenses, even the Xerox bills, and his partners grew very critical, so Cousin Houser assigned the case to the firm's newest associate, all six-feet-three-inches and 280 pounds of man named Rob Strasser, who endeared himself to all of us by believing totally in our cause and working on its behalf 24/7.

The lawsuit was emotionally demanding—I mean, it merely meant life or death—but we needed to run the business at the same time.

In the middle of the year we had to have our annual meeting with our Convertible Debenture holders. All fifteen of them came to Eugene, Oregon. We had, for the first time, lost money in the transition, so not unsurprisingly they unanimously expressed disappointment in the company's performance in general, and in me, its CEO, in particular. It was a tough afternoon for me, and as I drove home I thought that if we ever thought about going public—meaning hundreds of shareholders—if we ever thought of that, please shoot me.

1974

There was tons of tension as the trial opened in the Federal District Court in Portland, Oregon, in April. We all rose as the judge entered the room. He was perfect and a little scary. James Burns was sixty-ish and he had a severe countenance and the heaviest, darkest eyebrows you will ever see. He called himself "James the Just" and there would be no frivolity in that courtroom.

Our case was that while we said we would not sell competing shoes, with the change in ownership of the company Onitsuka said that they would not sell to our competitors. We said that we continued to act reasonably and that we were entitled to own the rights to the shoes and the shoe names.

Our performance in court reflected who we were: stumbling, inarticulate, and sincere.

Onitsuka's case was that Mr. Knight had actually asked to be taken over—were they serious?—and their communications about setting up competitors was really just market research.

After two intense weeks the trial closed. We felt pretty good about our case in general, but were concerned as well. In our view, Kitami had lied through his teeth, but "James the Just" seemed to be buying what he said. When Kitami stepped off the stand, the judge said, "Thank you very much, sir."

Thank you very much, sir? He never said that to me or any of our witnesses.

While this was going on, there was great news on the business front. The Waffle Trainer, which incorporated Bowerman's new waffle sole, was flying off the shelves, leading to an increase in annual sales from $4.8 million to $8.4 million and our first year of real profitability with Nike.

But it seemed every bit of good news was countered by negative: President Nixon changed the currency rate between the Japanese yen and the US dollar. Henceforth, instead of a pegged rate of 360 yen to the dollar, the ratio would float. In a year and half the rate went all the way down to 180 to 1. In other words, regardless of labor or raw materials cost, the cost of our shoes had doubled.

So it was like the good news/bad news jokes which were well liked at the time: We had a very popular product. We had no place to make it.

Just at that time we heard that "James the Just" had made his decision. We had to be at the courthouse for his ruling in two days.

I was incredibly tense as the judge entered the courtroom one last time.

His findings were short and simple: He found that Mr. Kitami had been untruthful in his testimony, that Nike was entitled to the names of the shoes we originated, and he would name a special master to determine what the money damages should be.

We won. We won. We would stay alive and get some money as well.

I shook Cousin Houser's hand. He had done a brilliant job in the courtroom. Then I hugged Strasser, buried in his bulk. We had been most fortunate to have this extremely bright, very hard-working man on our side.

And then I sent Jeff Johnson back to New England to see if we could manufacture shoes in the U.S.

1975

"Pay Nissho first!" It wasn't just a mantra. They were words we lived by.

Nissho had a subordinate position to the bank so that if disaster happened, the bank would get all of its money back before Nissho got a dime. Nissho had all the risk, so that the end of every month whatever money we had left from required payments went to Nissho. And the demands for cash were extreme. With the Waffle Trainer sales up we were en route to nearly doubling our sales again, which, particularly with the increasing costs, meant that our dollars in inventory were sky rocketing.

Jeff Johnson got a small shoe factory going in Exeter, New Hampshire. Costs were a little higher than they were at the time in Japan, but lower than what they would be in another year.

Jeff did ask one troubling question: "How are we going to pay for the factory?"

My answer: "Nissho will pay for it."

"Why would they do that?"

"We're not going to tell them."

"Oh."

So sometime at the end of the month we would "play the float." We would write Nissho a check which would create a temporary overdraft. Sales were growing to over million a month and an overdraft of $25,000 would be covered in one or two days.

Except in April we stretched the overdraft to $75,000 with bank accounts with warehouses and a couple retail outlets across the country. One banker bounced one check. Then they all bounced.

Hayes and I were called into the Bank of California for a meeting. It was serious. And very short. We were kicked out of the bank. The million dollars we owed them—and did not have—was due at once.

Gulp.

But I wasn't done. I had to walk up ten flights of stairs in the same building and inform Nissho that the one million I was supposed to pay them that month would be short—by about one million dollars. In addition I needed to borrow another million.

The ultimate decision on what Nissho would do was to be decided by Tadayuki Ito, finance manager.

He came out with Sumeragi and they audited our books for three days. In the course of the audit, they, of course, discovered our hidden factory, which took about a full hour to explain. But through a series of stumbling, disjointed explanations, it was a hedge against no factory source at all in Japan. Ito, who never showed any emotion, and wore a very severe demeanor through that whole difficult hour, at the end he nodded and said, "Let's move on." I swear he looked at me and gave me a small smile.

But then it turned out that the debt of three or four million which we thought showed on our books was not showing on our books. After much effort to chase down the discrepancy it turned out that, unbeknownst to any of us at Nike, Sumeragi was hiding invoices in his desk drawer to make our debt look less high.

"Why in the world would you do this?" Ito asked his friend and coworker.

"Because," Sumeragi said, "I work with these people every day. I have met Steve Prefontaine, I helped them move, I helped when extra shipments were needed from the warehouse. I think someday this can be a big company. Nike is my business child."

I sat back dumbfounded. It was emotionally understandable, but in a U.S. company, it could wind up putting him in prison. But Ito just stared, then gave that small smile that I had seen on disclosing the factory.

The following day Ito, Hayes and I had a meeting with senior officials at the Bank of California, the people that had made the decision to kick us out.

Another brief meeting: "We are here to pay off Nike's entire loan in full," I announced.

"In full," Ito echoed.

Ito handed the bankers a check. They looked at it. They paused for quite a long time and then said, "It will be deposited the first thing tomorrow morning."

Ito was very firm. "It will be deposited right now."

"Yes, you are right. Right now."

"And by the way . . . I believe your bank has been negotiating in San Francisco to be one of Nissho's bankers."

"Yes," they said eagerly.

"Well, I must tell you that it will be a waste of your time to pursue those negotiations further."

"Are you sure?"

"Quite!"

I slid my eyes toward Hayes. I tried not to smile. I tried very hard. I failed.

Memorial weekend followed and I don't know if I'd ever needed a break more. There was to be a great track meet in Eugene. Steve Prefontaine had arranged a six-event meet. Finland had the world record holder in the discus and he would come and compete with Oregon's Mac Wilkins, a world class thrower in his own right. But the main event would be the 5,000 rematch of the Olympics—between gold medalist Lasse Viren and Pre.

But at the last moment, Viren cancelled. With a sold-out Hayward Field guaranteed, Pre desperately reached out to

Olympic marathon gold medalist Frank Shorter, who accepted.

It was a great race. Pre, who always led, could not take the lead. Shorter held him off until the last 200. Pre dug deep and won by five yards to a wildly cheering stadium.

Penny and I drove back to Portland knowing we had, one more time, seen a great Prefontaine race.

At five the next morning my phone rang. Never a good sign, but it was 8 a.m. in Exeter. I thought it was probably Johnson with some production problem.

But it was not Johnson. It was Geoff Hollister. It was hard to understand him. He was crying. After a post meet party at Geoff's house, Pre had driven Shorter to his hotel, and on the way home swerved to avoid an oncoming car, and crashed into a huge boulder on the side of the road. The car had flipped over. Pre was dead.

1976

The good news was sales (led by Bowerman's Waffle Trainer) kept booming. But elsewhere there were problems, most of which related to the predicted increased value of the Japanese yen.

Our little Exeter factory could help somewhat, but it could not generate the volume needed, so after much surveying we focused on a new country: Taiwan. Taiwan had hundreds of small factories, so we should be able to get some of the better ones to work on our high-quality shoes. It was a good theory, but we had trouble finding the right partner. Finally, after touring many of the shoe areas, Jim Gorman and I stumbled on a small factory in Doeleho, a small town just outside of Taichung. Feng Tai was its name and it was making hundreds of thousand of low-quality sports shoes, but its owner CH Wong expressed hearftfelt desire to improve and work with us. He was a man of complete disclosure and showed us everything about his factory. Everything except one room.

"What's in there?" I questioned insistently.

Finally, he said, "That's where I live with my wife and two children."

Gorman volunteered to move to Taiwan to oversee quality control. Our Taiwan adventure was underway. The partnership with Feng Tai worked out pretty well. It is the cornerstone of our Asia production, and CH Wong has multiple factories all over Asia now. His company is listed on the Taiwan stock exchange.

With Taiwan and Exeter we had a strategy—in its early stages to be sure—to offset the continuing rise of the Japanese currency.

1976 was another Olympic year. By then we had four years experience with our new line, and although it was still young we had a complete complement of spiked and flat running shoes.

Once again the Olympic trials were in our backyard—Eugene, Oregon. In 1972 no wearer of Nike shoes made the Olympic team. In the first event in 1976, all three qualifiers, led by Frank Shorter, wore Nike shoes. Through the rest of the trials we dominated the distance races and were very excited about the games which were to be held in Montreal, Canada.

Monetary endorsements were now legal by Olympic rules and we put almost all of our budget on Shorter. He had liked the shoes, he liked Hollister, and since he was the defending Olympic marathon champion, we saw him as the logical successor to Pre.

We were very excited for the start of the marathon. We had won no medals at these games but Shorter was favored in the marathon.

But when he lined up at the starting line, he was not in our shoes. He was in his old shoes—Tigers, the guys that we had fought a war with in the courtroom.

Hollister was devastated. Me too.

And then Shorter got beat by an East German in Adidas shoes. It didn't make it better. It made it worse.

It was a double defeat. We had bet most of our budget on Shorter. But it was an emotional investment, too. We liked him. We had hoped he would be the new Pre.

I never exactly understood Shorter's last-minute switch.

He said there was a tear in the upper near the sole and that they didn't feel right. I don't know. I still feel part of it was that he was nervous about wearing new shoes when the old ones had won Olympic gold.

With these various mixed results our management met to plan the new year at Sun River, Oregon.

During the course of the meeting, Jeff Johnson looked around the room at his peers and observed, "This is the only top management in the world, where someone could look at the room and yell, 'Hey Buttface,' and every person would think he was talking to him."

The name caught on, and top managers called themselves that for the next seven or eight years. It was really an acknowledgment that we were all a group of misfits. But we were misfits on a mission.

1977

The business was constantly surprising. In the spring of 1977 I got a phone call from a man claiming to be a former Rockwell aerospace engineer. He had a shoe design he wanted to show me.

"C'mon up," I answered. His name was Frank Rudy and he was a very serious man.

His invention was an air midsole for running shoes. It had

been tried before. The problem with previous designs was that the air always leaked out of the bag so the midsole would go flat after one long run. Frank Rudy insisted he had invented a way around that problem.

He made his pitch in a room with Strasser, Hayes, and me. "So," I said, "I got time for a six-mile run before dinner."

"There is no moderator," Rudy responded, meaning there was nothing to control the midsole—it would just flop around underneath the foot.

"Nevermind," I said. "I will get the idea."

I found the run wobbly, as promised, but sensational. We had an agreement that evening, and now forty years later we have sold some 400 million pairs of air-soled shoes. Sometimes it pays to pick up the phone.

Later we received a call from another shoe inventor. His name was Sonny Vacarro. After the Frank Rudy experience, I was eager to see what he had.

Sonny Vacarro's invention was some sort of hydro architectural beast that got laughed out of the room. But in the course of his pitch Sonny mentioned he had access to every college basketball coach in the country through his Dapper Dan All-Star Basketball Classic, which annually featured the top thirty players in the country.

"You really have access to all those coaches?" I asked.

So we hired him as a consultant to put together our first

coaches club, a group of the best coaches we could get. Most of the famous ones were already under contract to either Adidas or Converse, so we went after the leftovers.

They weren't bad. We signed hall-of-famers John Thompson, Eddie Sutton, Jerry Tarkanian, Lute Olson, Jim Valvano, George Raveling, and Lou Carnesecca. They became the cornerstone of our college basketball program.

We were not the only ones who were hurt by the changing Japanese currency. The many low-cost shoes made in Japan had to find a new home. That home was Korea. Overnight, huge factories sprouted to fill the demand now that factories in Japan cost too much. These factories were more like little cities. Each of the big five factories in Pusan had 12,000 employees.

But low-cost shoes have to be upgraded to make our product, and at such size they were not about to accommodate little old us. But now we were producing over a million pairs a year. So we started a Korea program, and were delighted to find the cooperation of the big five factories. Three years later they were our biggest source.

So things were percolating pretty well, and I was sitting at my desk fat, dumb, and happy when in the morning mail was an envelope with a return address from U.S. Customs. Innocent looking enough.

Inside was an invoice: for past due U.S. Customs duties for $25 million. Our annual sales—before cost of goods and all expenses—were $24 million.

I immediately called Strasser, who had recently joined the company full time, into my office. "This has to be some kind of joke."

"I'll find out," he said.

One day later he came back with the bad news. "This is no joke. It seems there is a 1932 law applying to Benzedrine chemicals, cherry stone clams, and sneakers, that allows duties to be applied not to cost, as customs had always done and written us a letter saying they would continue to do, but based on the U.S. selling price of a like or similar manufactured U.S. made shoe. It seems some U.S. factories had lobbied Customs convincing them that their shoes were like or similar so our duties should be doubled. Retroactively."

"The shoes have already been sold. The duty bill already paid. There is no way we can pay this."

"Guess we better fight."

1977 brought a personal event that would never even be a footnote in company history, but it meant something to me.

During our nightly phone call, my father asked about my day and his two grandsons. Then he asked, "Did you get home in time to see the Clippers vs. Rockets game?"

"No I didn't."

"There was a terrible event. Kermit Washington slugged Rudy Tomjanovich so hard it might have killed him. It was awful. . . ." After a long pause, he said, "But you should have seen the close-up of the shoes."

And there it was. From a father so understated in handing out praise that it didn't happen—a compliment. Translation: the switch from CPA to sneaker salesman, well, you did okay, son.

1978

We needed to do everything possible to fight the customs ruling on American Selling Price (ASP).

To start with, it would be a full-time job. Strasser suggested we hire Rich Werschkul from Cousin Houser's law firm. Werschkul was tired of insurance law and gratefully accepted, but Cousin Houser extracted a pledge from me: I would not make any more hires from his firm.

The choice of Werschkul couldn't have been better. He had a Bachelor's degree from Stanford, had gone to University of Oregon Law school, wore black horn-rimmed glasses that he adjusted every thirty seconds, dressed like a New England prep school student, and, best of all, became obsessed with our cause.

Our fight was in Washington, D.C., so he moved there. He made fast friends with politicians, petitioned, lobbied, and pleaded our cause with passion if not always with sanity. Day after day he ran up and down the halls of Congress, handing out free pairs of Nike's shoes. The politicians gave back a unanimous message: Give me something in writing, son, something I can study.

So he did. *Werschkul on American Selling Price, Volume I.* Several hundred pages, but what really scared you was the *Volume I.*

When occasionally he would find an unsympathetic listener, Werschkul would simply go postal: "Don't you people realize," he shouted, "that freedom is on trial here? FREEDOM! Did you know that Hitler's father was a customs inspector?"

So the fight was on. And it was going to go the whole fifteen rounds. It could take years.

ASP dominated everything. One more time: if we lost this there would be no company.

But there was bright news. Sales were booming and Rudy's first air-sole shoes hit the market. We had some problems with the quality of the new material in the upper, but the consensus in the running community was, "What a ride."

1979

If ASP dominated 1978, it also dominated 1979. Werschkul had opened some doors, but found that to be effective on this big a case, the CEO would have to be there to plead our case. So I began commuting to D.C.

I started with the Assistant Secretary of Treasury, the overseer of U.S. Customs.

I began by handing him a document. "You have right here," I said, "a memo stating that the American Selling Price does not apply to Nike shoes. The memo comes from the U.S. Treasury."

"Hmmm," the bureau-kraken said. He looked it over and pushed it back at me. "That is not binding on customs."

In other words, my government lied to me. Like a modified line from the movie *Animal House*: "You screwed up. You trusted us."

Gritting my teeth, I said, "This whole case is nothing but the result of a dirty trick played by our competitors. We're being penalized for our success."

"We don't see it that way."

"By we ... who do you mean?"

"The U.S. government."

Well, I was not going to give up. We would fight. But we had a formidable, big opponent.

We started with the Oregon delegation, and were very fortunate that Congressman Al Ullman was the chairman of the House Ways and Means Committee, Senator Mark Hatfield was the chairman of Appropriations, and Senator Bob Packwood was the chairman of Finance.

We lobbied very hard and they expressed a strong desire to help.

And then many others were also there to help: Tom Foley, Speaker of the House, from the state of Washington, who had a certain affinity for fellow Northwesterners; Senators Al Gore and Jim Sasser from Tennessee, where we had a big warehouse; and Bill Cohen and George Mitchell from Maine, where we had expanded factory operations after outgrowing Exeter.

In the fall of 1979 I had my second meeting with the bureau-kraken.

"I'm sick and tired," he said, "of hearing from your high-placed friends."

"Well," I said, "you'll be hearing from them until this situation is resolved."

Taiwan and Korea were humming now, which was a good thing because Japan had completely priced itself out of the market. Not that Japan was suffering economically. Its automobiles and electronics had more than made up for the loss of shoe exports.

But Taiwan and Korea prices were now rising quickly. What would happen if they became uneconomical for shoes, like Japan? We had no backup.

So, on my annual swing through Asian factories, I decided

to visit China for the first time. Nixon had started the thaw in relations between the two countries and now Jimmy Carter had recognized it.

I sat in a hotel in Hong Kong for three days waiting for my visa. It never came.

When explaining this at our board meeting, Chuck Robinson, who had recently consented to be a member, and the Allen Group, headed by Henry Kissinger's brother Walter, who had tried to get business going in China, were there. When Walter wanted to get the Allen group into China, he had not called his brother, he had called his Princeton classmate David Chang, who had succeeded.

I called Chang.

1980

At the first Buttface meeting of the year I said, "How 'bout this . . . obviously I have been thinking about this a lot. We have a shoe factory in the United States. What we need to do is . . . American Selling Price *ourselves.*"

Everybody laughed. Properly. It was such an absurd suggestion.

Then stopped and looked at each other. Maybe an absurd response to such an absurd law could work.

We started manufacturing a limited number of knock-offs

of our Nike shoes, which we branded the One Line, selling them at the most narrow profit. There was no more 'like or similar' shoe than that.

U.S. Customs never argued. It immediately reduced our duties, not to what they would be if based on Asia factory costs, but below what we were getting from those other U.S. made shoes.

Then we produced a TV ad telling the story of a little company in Oregon fighting the big, bad government. It opened with a runner doing his lonely road work, as a deep voice extolled the ideals of patriotism, liberty, the American way, and fighting tyranny. It got people fired up.

Then we delivered the final move. On February 29, 1980, we filed a $25 million antitrust suit in U.S. District Court for the Southern District of New York, alleging that our competitors and assorted rubber companies, through underhanded business practices, had conspired to take us out.

It didn't take long. The bureau-kraken's bosses called to begin settlement talks.

They came down from $25 million to $9 million. Now that we over $200 million in sales, we could pay. But we shouldn't have to. We relied on our government's word when we imported those shoes. But Chuck Robinson pointed out this was government, this was a negotiation, and they were not going to settle at $0.

I took the offer of $9 million.

The battle over ASP was over.

Chuck Robinson also pointed out that with ASP out of the way, there was nothing stopping us from going public. "And," he said, "to get over your control issues, I think we can go public with two classes of stock which would allow current insiders to maintain control."

"If you can do that . . . well, that would change a lot of things."

There was no time to rest. In late 1979, David Chang had sent a letter with fifty pages of exhibits requesting an invitation to visit factories in China. After five months, we received an answer. Our six-person entourage was invited to the People's Republic of China in July. That would be the hottest month of the year there.

The selected six: David Chang, Hayes, Strasser, Neil Lauridsen (head of Taiwan factories), Harry Carsh (head of our Maine factory), and me.

Our handlers met us at the Beijing Airport and never let us out their sights. They took us by train to remote towns, far from Beijing, where we saw vast and terrifying industrial complexes and small factories, each one more outdated than the last. They were old, rusty, and decrepit.

Above all, they were filthy. A shoe would roll off the

assembly line with a stain, a swath of grime, and nothing would be done. There was no overarching sense of cleanliness, no real quality control. When we pointed out a defective shoe, the officials would shrug and say, "Perfectly functional."

The Chinese didn't see why the nylon or canvas in a pair of shoes needed to be the same shade in the left shoe and right. It was common for a left shoe to be light blue and right to be dark blue.

This is what we had to work with. But it seemed to me that we should try.

The final discussions would be in Shanghai. We had a second goal there: We would meet with the Ministry of Sports to make a deal for their track and field team.

Unlike the Western world, where every athlete made his own deal, the Chinese government negotiated endorsement deals for all its athletes. So, in an old Shanghai schoolhouse, in a classroom with seventy-five-year-old furniture under a huge portrait of Chairman Mao, Strasser and I met with the ministry representative.

For several minutes the representative lectured us on the beauties of communism. He went on and on, and said that they preferred to do business with like-minded people. Strasser and I looked at each other. Then he stopped his lecture, leaned forward, and asked in a low voice, "How much you willing to pay?"

Within two hours, we had a deal. Four years later in Los Angeles, the Chinese track and field team would walk into an

Olympic Stadium for the first time in twenty-five years, and they would be wearing Nike track shoes and warm-ups.

Our final meeting was with the Ministry of Foreign Trade. As with the previous meeting, there were several rounds of long speeches, mainly by officials. Hayes was bored during the first round. By the third he was suicidal. He started playing with the loose threads on the front of his polyester dress shirt. Suddenly he became annoyed with the threads. He took out his lighter. As the deputy minister of foreign trade was hailing us as worthy partners, he stopped and look up to see that Hayes had set himself on fire. He beat out the flame with his hands, and managed to put it out, but only after ruining the moment and the speaker's mojo.

It didn't matter. Just before getting on the plane home we signed deals with two Chinese factories, and officially became the first American shoemaker in twenty-five years to be allowed to do business in China.

We barely had time to unpack. The public offering was about to be a reality. We polled different investment banks—all were on board with two classes of stock, which would allow the insiders to maintain control. Of all the firms we picked Kuhn Loeb, where Chuck Robinson had previously been vice president, to head up the offering.

We had to get Securities and Exchange Commission

approval. It took fifty drafts of the prospectus until it was approved and looked and sounded the way we wanted.

Then came the road show. Meetings with investment bankers began at a breakfast meeting in New York City.

Our presentation was not polished, but it was enthusiastic, sincere, and our numbers were pretty good.

We covered eight cities and ten meetings in five days. Hayes, Johnson, and I made the pitch to investment bankers. It was intense and exhausting, especially coming on the heels of the China trip.

We still had to price the offering after everything else was done, so we set the offering date: December 2, 1980.

On that date, Hayes and I were on the speaker phones with Bob Macy of Kuhn Loeb, and he announced, "We cannot go any higher than twenty-one dollars."

The range during the road show was 18–22. I thought the road show had gone as well as we could have hoped. The difference between 21 and 22 was a million dollars to the company.

"Our number is 22," I said.

There were several voices talking on the other side. Then they said, "We can go to $21.50. That is our final offer."

"Our number is 22. If you can't go that high, we don't go."

Cracking silence. Coughing. Papers being shuffled. After an eternity, "I'm sorry, we will have to call you back."

Click.

Five minutes.

Then fifteen.

The phone rang. We pushed the speaker button. Bob Macy spoke, "Gentlemen . . . we have a deal. We will send it out to market on Friday."

I drove home. The boys were outside playing. Penny was standing in the kitchen. "How was your day?" she asked.

"Okay," I said.

"Great."

"We got our price."

She smiled. "Of course you did."

I woke up the next morning to a cold and rainy day. I went to the window. The trees were dripping water. The world was the same as it had been the day before, and yet I was rich.

I ate breakfast and then I drove to work. I was at my desk before anyone else.

Epilogue

A Final Letter to the Young Reader

Nike is an adult now. There is much to be proud of and many things to be sad about, and lots that happened after going public in 1980.

There are some evenings when I sit in my office and look out at the lighted running trails through the woods and think about so many parts of the journey.

One of my favorite memories is this one:

In 1976 Bob Woodell's mother came to me and said, "I know you are always stretched for cash, and I just wanted you to know the family has savings of seven thousand dollars and we will loan it to you if you need it."

I was stunned. Finally I managed, "Why would you do that?"

"Well," she said, "if you can't trust the company your son is working for, then who can you trust?"

I really didn't want to use it, but a year later we were desperate, and I told Bob if the offer was still good, the company really needed the loan. Which was given the next day.

The loan was still outstanding five years later when we went public, and the company allowed them to convert the loan into common stock.

The loan became public traded stock worth $1.8 million. Merle Woodell called her grown daughter Carol and announced, "We're millionaires. My son Bob told me so."

The public offering gave us another opportunity as well. We had paid Carolyn Davidson thirty-five dollars for designing the winger swoosh logo. With offering, we invited her back to the office and gave her five hundred shares of stock, which she has never sold and is now worth $1 million.

The China Trip

The China trip in 1980 paid big dividends. China in the coming years became our largest source of footwear, with about 40 percent of our worldwide production, and perhaps more importantly it became our second-biggest, and fastest-growing, market (second to the United States).

It Is Not "Just a Business"

There has been so much personal interaction with fellow workers—teammates rather than employees—and with customers and factories and athletes. With LeBron giving me an inscribed Rolex made in 1972 when Nike was formed, to Alberto Salazar having a heart attack and asking me to look after Galen Rupp if he didn't survive, to sitting with the family at the funeral of Michael Jordan's father.

I think of that phrase "It's just a business." It's never just a business. It never will be. If it does become just business, that will mean that business is very bad.

Deaths of Matt, Bowerman, and Rob

The years passed and prove that time is not endless, that man is mortal.

For me the saddest moment was the drowning of my son Matthew in a diving accident in El Salvador in 2004.

There is almost nothing sadder than the death of a child. It comes with an emptiness that never leaves. I curl up in a ball as I write this.

More than a decade after his death, the person I live with leaves the TV on all night. Its flickering light breaks up the darkness, and the constant drone from the corner of the room is a comfort to her.

And yet for all the sadness, it has come with a single positive: It drives home, with the force of a baseball bat, just how precious is the life of a child. For me that means, one more time, those grandchildren.

Bill Bowerman, my old coach, died on Christmas Eve in 1999 in Fossil, Oregon, the town of his childhood.

After his longtime friend and neighbor John Jaqua had called with the news, it took me an hour to come out of my den. I gave up on Kleenex and just draped a towel over my shoulder, a move I learned from another beloved coach—John Thompson.

Rob Strasser passed suddenly too. Heart attack, 1993, age forty-six. He was so young, it was a tragedy, all the more so because it came after we'd had a falling out. We just clashed too many times, and he quit.

It might have been okay if he'd just quit. But he went to work for Adidas. I felt this as a terrible betrayal that took me more than a decade to forgive. But the circle has a way of rounding. Recently—happily, proudly—Nike hired his daughter Avery. Twenty-two years old, she works in Special Events and she is thriving. It's a blessing and a joy to see her name in the company directory.

Foreign Factories

I felt the same sense of betrayal when Nike came under attack for conditions in our overseas factories—the so-called sweatshop controversy. Whenever reporters said a factory was unsatisfactory, they never said how much better it was than the day we first went in. They never said how hard we'd worked with our factory partners to upgrade conditions, to make them safer and cleaner. They never said those factories weren't ours, that we were renters, one among many tenants. They simply searched until they found a worker with complaints and conditions, and they used that worker to vilify us, and only us, knowing our name would generate maximum publicity.

But finally we knew we could do better, and we would. We told the world: Just watch. We'll make our factories shining examples.

And we did. In the ten years since the bad headlines and lurid exposés, we've used the crisis to reinvent the entire company.

For instance: One of the worst things about a shoe factory used to be the rubber room, where uppers and soles are bonded. The fumes are choking, toxic, cancer causing. So we invented a water-based bonding agent that gives off no fumes, thereby eliminating 7 percent of the carcinogens in the air. Then we gave this invention to our competitors, handed it over to anyone who wanted it.

They all did. Nearly all of them now use it.

Out of the sweatshop crisis also came the Girl Effect, a massive Nike effort to break the generational cycles of povery in the bleakest corners of the world. Along with the United Nations and other corporate and government partners, the Girl Effect is spending tens of millions of dollars in a smart, tough, global campaign to educate and connect and lift up young girls. Economists and sociologists, not to mention our own hearts, tell us that, in many societies, young girls are the most economically vulnerable and vital demographic. So helping them helps all. Whether striving to end child marriage in Ethiopia, or building safe spaces for teenage girls in Nigeria, or launching a magazine and radio show that deliver powerful, inspiring messages to young Rwandans, the Girl Effect is changing millions of lives, and the best days of my week, month, year are those when I receive the glowing reports from its front lines.

I close with advice that might be helpful to young readers of this book. In some ways you are all my grandchildren.

How best to prepare for the battles that lie before you?

A. There is not a clear path in life.

Which makes it all the more interesting.

Work with what you have. You don't have to be twenty-four and unemployed. Tell the world you are the CEO of Blue Ribbon Sports.

B. Do what you know and love. (Like running.)

You will have dark days even when you do this. If you don't, the dark days can become intolerable.

C. Work hard.

Luck plays a big role, yes. Some people may not call it luck. They might call it Tao, or Spirit. Or God.

But put it this way: The harder you work, the better your

Tao. And since no one has ever defined Tao, I still go to Mass. Have faith in yourself but also have faith in faith. Not faith as others define it. Faith as you define it.

D. Don't be shy about asking for advice.

In my travels I have occasionally met promising young people who insist they are not going to ask for help along the way. They want to do it themselves.

My approach was the opposite. It is hard enough out there: Get all the help you can. Getting help is just a part of that life-long search for wisdom.

E. Do work that means something to you.

Your goal should not be to seek a job, or even a career, but to seek a calling.

F. Realize that teamwork matters.

Two people of good talent working together will always beat two people of great talent who are not working together.

G. When the door is slammed on your dreams, look outside all that the world sees as normal.

If you can't get financing in this country, don't be afraid to look for it seven thousand miles from home.

H. There is such a thing as managing creativity.

Creative people have a tendency to be unpredictable, eccentric even. Some people throw up their hands and say, "That person is unmanageable." Look for nontraditional ways to manage that person.

I. And most important of all: Dare to take chances, lest you leave your talent buried in the ground.

Where there is no struggle there can be no art.

Six decades ago Frank Shallenberger, beloved professor of entrepreneurship at Stanford, said the words that meant so much to me, the words that became the mantra for his class, and my attitude:

"The only time you must not fail . . . is the last time you try."

It is my deepest hope that your journey is a joyous one.

Best,

Phil Knight

ACKNOWLEDGMENTS

I've spent a fair portion of my life in debt. As a young entrepreneur I became distressingly familiar with that feeling of going to sleep each night, waking up each day, owing many people a sum far greater than I could repay.

Nothing, however, has made me feel quite so indebted as the writing of this book.

Just as there's no end to my gratitude, there seems no proper, logical place to begin to express it. And so. At Nike, I wish to thank my assistant, Lisa McKillips, for doing everything—I mean everything— perfectly, cheerfully, and always with her dazzling smile; old friends Jeff Johnson and Bob Woodell for making me remember, and being patient when I remembered it different; historian Scott Reames for deftly sifting facts from myths; and Maria Eitel for applying her expertise to weightiest matters.

Of course, my biggest and most emphatic thanks to the 68,000 Nike employees worldwide for their daily efforts and their dedication, without which there would be no book, no author, no nothing. At Stanford, I wish to thank the mad genius and gifted teacher Adam Johnson for his golden example of what it means to be a working writer and a friend; Abraham Verghese, who instructs as he writes—quietly, effortlessly; and numberless graduate students I met with while sitting in the back row of writing classes—each inspired me with his or her passion for language and craft.

At Scribner, thanks to the legendary Nan Graham for her steadfast support; Brian Belfiglio, Roz Lippel, Susan Moldow, and Carolyn Reidy for their bracing, energizing enthusiasm; Kathleen Rizzo for keeping production moving smoothly forward while always maintaining a sublime calm; above all, thanks to my supremely talented and razor-sharp editor, Shannon Welch, who gave me the affirmation I needed, when I needed it, without either of us fully appreciating how much I needed it. Her early note of praise and analysis and precocious wisdom was everything.

Randomly, in no order, thanks to the many pals and colleagues who were so lavish with their time, talent, and advice, including super agent Bob Barnett, poet-administrator extraordinaire Eavan Boland, Grand Slam memoirist Andre Agassi, and number artist Del Hayes. A special and profound thank-you to memoirist-novelist-journalist-sportswriter-muse-friend J. R. Moehringer, whose generosity and good humor and enviable storytelling gifts I relied on through the many, many drafts of this book.

Last, I wish to thank my family, all of them, but particularly my son Travis, whose support and friendship meant—and mean—the world. And, of course, a full-throated, full-hearted thanks to my Penelope, who waited. And waited. She waited while I journeyed, and she waited while I got lost. She waited night after night while I made my maddeningly slow way home—usually late, the dinner cold—and she waited the last few years while I relived it all, aloud, and in my head, and on the page, even though there were parts she didn't care to relive. From the start, going on half a century, she's waited, and now at last I can hand her these hard-fought pages and say, about them, about Nike, about everything: "Penny, I couldn't have done it without you."

READING GROUP GUIDE

SHOE DOG

Young Readers Edition

By Phil Knight

About the Book

In this young readers edition of *Shoe Dog*, Phil Knight takes us on a remarkable journey of his experience "getting lost to find his way." Filled with stories, anecdotes, risks, and setbacks, we learn how a simple mission to import high-quality running shoes leads to one of the most successful brands ever. The journey is honest and filled with mistakes, struggles, and sacrifice. Following his own advice—"You must forget your limits," and "Just keep going. Don't stop."—Knight builds a reputation and brand with determination and heart that is exciting for young readers to learn about. His journey will also inspire young readers to believe in themselves, to hold on to hopes and dreams, and to strive to make their own dreams a reality.

Discussion Questions

1. What do you think the title of the book means? Why is the title important, and what might this tell us about Phil Knight? Do you recognize the logo? The adult version of this book has a black cover. Why is the young readers edition orange? Does the color make a difference?

2. What is a memoir? How is it different from a biography or autobiography? What's the difference between a memoir and a story? Why do we tell stories? Do you feel that storytelling is important? How often can your story change? Who knows your story best?

3. There are several main themes in this story, including resilience, perseverance, determination, courage, and hope. Can you name others? As you're reading, note the page number and paragraph and why these themes are evident in the text sample you've chosen. Keep a running chart or log of passages that demonstrate these themes.

4. Consider the qualities of a good leader; some leaders might be your principal, a teacher, a president, or a community member. What qualities does a good leader demonstrate? Does Knight show good leadership as he is trying to build his company? Why or why not? Cite examples from the book and other reputable sources.

5. Knight's memoir is a reflection on his life and discovering himself. In what ways does he tell his story so that it reflects who he is and what has shaped him? Make a chart of major events that shaped him throughout his journey.

6. Knight talks about the difference between wanting to win and not wanting to lose. Is there a difference? What do you think he means by this?

7. What does it mean "to get lost to find your way"? Cite examples from the story to support your answer.

8. In the chapter titled "1962," Knight decides to explore the world. Make a chart of the places he visits, what he does in each place, and the people he encounters. There are also several Zen and Buddhist sayings that helped him along the way; include those sayings on the chart as well. Compare and contrast what he has learned at each

place. He specifically asks, "Why am I here? What is my purpose?" Explain how this journey helps him, pointing out some defining moments and why you think they are important to his life.

9. An eclectic mix of people helped Knight get started: a former track star now paralyzed, an overweight accountant, and a salesman who was excessive in his letter writing. What did they have in common, and what were their differences? Why might such a group of people make a company so successful? Create a character chart showing the qualities you notice about the people Knight surrounded himself with. Consider their thoughts, plans, words, feelings, deeds, actions, strengths, and weaknesses.

10. Knight paid an art student thirty-five dollars to design a logo for his new company. Little did he realize that the "swoosh" would become so widely recognized. Why do you think this logo was so successful? What is it that appeals to people? If you had to design a logo for Nike (or any other shoe brand), what would you choose and why?

11. At one point, Knight talks about the letter of the law versus the spirit of the law. What does this mean? How does this conflict with what you may have been taught? Can you find

other examples in the book, in your own life, or in current news where rules have been broken for a good cause? Is this the right thing to do? Why or why not?

12. What do you think motivated Knight to share his story? How did you respond to his voice? What is Knight trying to achieve in telling us his story? Find examples of techniques he used to help achieve his goal. For example, using flashback to increase tension or repeating a line to support a theme.

13. Discuss the book's structure; each chapter is a year up until 1972. What changed for Knight at this point? What is his purpose in formatting the book like this? How did the author's use of language and his writing style keep you engaged? Does the author tell his story with comedy, self-pity, or something else? Find examples in the book that support your answer.

14. Knight includes a letter to his grandchildren at the beginning of the book. Why is this important? What do we learn about Knight from these personal reflections? Would the book be the same without the letter? Why or why not? If you received a letter from your grandfather, what would you do with it? How might it become a part of your life?

15. Knight makes several statements in the first part of the book titled "Dawn." He says his journey is messy, and that mistakes were made. He states that "you must forget your limits." Take one or two moments from this chapter that resonate with you. How can you apply this to your life right now, and the journey you are on? Define success and what it looks like in this book. What do you think success will look like for you?

16. In the epilogue, Knight shares a final letter with the reader. How does this letter give the reader a window into his state of mind? Why do you think he felt it was important to include this epilogue and the information he had learned?

17. Some say that survival is 80 percent mental (keeping a positive attitude), 10 percent skill (knowledge), and 10 percent equipment. Why is Knight's survival important to this story? What has he taught us? How did he deal with his drive, the pressure, and conflict? What resources did he use? What can you take with you from reading about his mistakes and journey as you move on with your own journey?

18. LeBron James, Kobe Bryant, Michael Jordan, Tiger Woods, April Holmes, Maria Sharapova—all these

star athletes are sponsored by Nike. What qualities do they have that reflect the Nike brand? Who else would you choose? Are there other athletes who have Nike sponsorship? If so, who are they?

19. If you could design a new logo for Nike, what would it be and why? If you could design a new book cover for *Shoe Dog*, what would you choose and why? Draw your designs and explain what they mean, and how they relate to Knight's story.

20. The four-minute mile barrier was first broken in 1954. What is the current record, and when was it set? What kind of training does it take to be able to run a four-minute mile or less? What is involved both physically and mentally? What science is involved in running at this pace? Try running a mile. Is it difficult or easy to do? Keep a running journal and note how long it takes for you to run a mile. What happens as you track your pace over time? Why do you think this is?

21. What is involved in shoe design? How have science and technology changed the way shoes are designed and made? Create a chart of all the different kinds of shoes (starting with Tiger) that Knight had to create to get to

something he felt was truly new and different. Include things like the Waffle, spikes, materials, etc. Create a new shoe that might be of interest to Nike. What would it look like? How would you design, create, test, and present this shoe to someone like Knight? Present your new shoe to your group and explain why you think your shoe would be a good fit for Nike.

This Reading Group Guide is taken from the Curriculum Guide, written in alignment with the Common Core Standards (www.corestandards.org), that is provided by Simon & Schuster for classroom, library, and reading group use and available with our other Reading Group Guides at simonandschustser. net. This guide may be reproduced in its entirety or excerpted for educational purposes.
Curriculum Guide written in 2017 by Sharon Haupt, District Librarian, San Luis Coastal Unified School District.

Looking for another great book?
Find it
IN THE MIDDLE.

Fun, fantastic books for kids
in the in-be**TWEEN** age.

IntheMiddleBooks.com